Handbook for Widows

JUNE HEMER
founder of the National Association of Widows

ANN STANYER
Department of Applied Social Studies, Lanchester Polytechnic

with contributions from
Mary Stott, O.B.E. and Robert Zara, Ll.B

Virago
London

Acknowledgements

We should like to thank all those widows who have given us the experience necessary to write this pamphlet; the Voluntary Services Unit of the Home Office for the generous grant which facilitated the research for and writing of the handbook; the Chase Charity and Charities Aid Foundation for grants for the purpose of printing drafts; and the Trustees, for their guidance and enthusiasm.

Published by Virago Limited 1978
4th floor, 5 Wardour Street, London W1V 3HE

Reprinted 1978

copyright © 1978 Widows Advisory Trust

ISBN 0 86068 033 9

Printed and bound by Unwin Brothers Limited,
The Gresham Press, Old Woking, Surrey

VIRAGO
is a feminist publishing company:

'It is only when women start to organize in large numbers that we
become a political force, and begin to move towards the possibility
of a truly democratic society in which every human being can be
brave, responsible, thinking and diligent in the struggle to live at
once freely and unselfishly'

SHEILA ROWBOTHAM
Women, Resistance and Revolution

VIRAGO
Advisory Group

Andrea Adam
Carol Adams
Sally Alexander
Anita Bennett
Liz Calder
Bea Campbell
Angela Carter
Mary Chamberlain
Deirdre Clark
Anna Coote
Jane Cousins
Bobbie Crosby
Nicci Crowther
Anna Davin
Rosalind Delmar
Zoe Fairbairns

Carolyn Faulder
Jane Gregory
Christine Jackson
Suzanne Lowry
Jean McCrindle
Mandy Merck
Cathy Porter
Spare Rib Collective
Mary Stott
Anne Summers (*Australia*)
Rosalie Swedlin
Michelene Wandor
Alison Weir
Elizabeth Wilson
Women and Education
Barbara Wynn

Contents

PREFACE

Preface

The **National Association of Widows** was founded by June Hemer in 1971 primarily as a pressure group designed to obtain an improved tax position and better pensions for widows. However, since that time the Association has developed beyond simply being a pressure group into an organization which aims to help widows NOW through its Widows' Advisory Service. There are over 5,000 members.

The Association is honoured to have Baroness MacLeod, widow of Ian MacLeod, as its President. All widows are eligible for membership and pay a small subscription. Each year a Council of 14 is elected from the membership to run the Association. There are nearly seventy branches scattered throughout England, Wales and Scotland. The number of branches has increased steadily over the years and will continue to do so whilst widows feel that they are neglected and unjustly treated. Many Members of Parliament and Members of the House of Lords actively support the Association—asking questions in the House of Commons, initiating debates in both Houses, trying to get Acts passed and trying to generally improve the position of widows in our society.

The Association produces a newsletter for its members, participates in television and radio programmes, has organized rallies to Parliament and encourages the formation of branches and local social activites.

But over the years the Association has found that even if it has achieved small improvements through its pressure on Parliament (such as persuading the Inland Revenue to publish a leaflet on income tax for widows and helping to gain the special tax concession for one-parent families) many widows need immediate help, help which has not been forthcoming either from other voluntary organizations or from the statutory social services. Often this help has not been forthcoming because what is needed most of all is a sympathetic ear from someone who has also experienced bereavement.

Therefore the Association formed the **Widows' Advisory Trust.** The Trust seeks to finance the setting up of local advisory services, services provided by widows for widows. The Trust also finances help for widows in areas where there is no local advisory service. Essentially this means covering the travelling, telephone and postage expenses of those giving advice. The use made of the **Widows Advisory Service** has increased to the extent that it is hoped that a national service will be available in the 1980's.

This Handbook has arisen out of the voluntary work done by the **National Association of Widows** and the **Widows Advisory Trust.** It brings together, for the first time in one short pamphlet, both a brief description of the main services available to widows and suggestions as to how to prevent or deal with the practical problems most frequently encountered during widowhood. The authors are most conscious of the fact that emotional problems are at least as important as practical problems and regret that the Handbook has had to be limited in its scope. However, we hope that you will find it helpful and that you will not hesitate to approach the Widows Advisory Service if your problems are not dealt with fully here.

If you would like to join the National Association of Widows and/or wish to obtain advice then write to Headquarters, NAW, c/o Voluntary Service Centre, Chell Road, Stafford, ST1 2QA or telephone Stafford (0785) 45465 or 56532.

There are branches of the National Association of Widows in the following areas:

Adlington & District (Lancashire)
Altringham and Sale
Astley Bridge, Bolton
Blackhall Colliery, Hartlepool
Brierley Hill
Brighton
Bury St. Edmunds
Cheadle
Chelmsley Wood
Chesterfield*
Coventry*
Dalry (Ayrshire)
Derby
Dudley
East Ham
East Kilbride*
Eston (Cleveland)
Gloucester
Gravesend and District
Great Wyrley
Guisborough
Handsworth and Perry Barr
Harrow
High Wycombe
Ilford
Ipswich
Kidsgrove
Kirkby and Ashfield
Leamington Spa
Leeds*
Liverpool
Loftus
Luton and District
Manchester

Mansfield*
Market Warsop
Middlesborough
Nelson
Nottingham
Nuneaton
Plumstead
Rossendale
Royal Forest of Dean
Saltburn-by-the-Sea
Scunthorpe
Sheffield Central
Sheffield Greenhill
Sheffield Park
South Elmsall and Pontefract
Southport
Stafford and Stone
Stevenage
Stockport
Stockton-on-Tees
Stoke-on-Trent
Stroud
Sutton Coldfield*
Trent Vale
Walsall
Wellington
West Wiltshire
Whitehaven
Wirral
Wolstanton
Wolverhampton
Worksop
Yardley

*These branches provide local advisory services.

Widowhood

In Britain there are over 3 million widows.

Although most widows are over sixty years of age widowhood is increasingly common among women who are under sixty. There are four times as many widows as widowers. Fifteen per cent of women are widows and yet our Welfare State does not face up either to this fact or its consequences. Lily Pincus writes 'However honestly it is faced, bereavement brings about a crisis of loss, probably the most severe crisis in human existence'. (*Death and the Family: the importance of mourning*).

In our society we tend to hide death. Clothes of mourning are no longer worn: blinds and curtains are no longer drawn in the home where someone has died. Funeral ceremonies may be hurried. Relatives may travel to the funeral and then return home the same day. There is a tendency in our society to produce 'brave' citizens, citizens who do not reveal their reactions, their feelings, their emotions.

Thus, not only are we ill-prepared to cope with death but we are not given an opportunity to mourn and to grieve openly, to adjust from being a wife to being a widow. More than 3 million of us have faced and overcome the most severe crisis in our life, against these odds. But the way has not been easy and society is not making it any easier.

We need time to cry, time to talk with someone who understands, time to grieve and to mourn. Dr Colin Murray Parkes writes of an 'optimal level' of grieving which varies from individual to individual: if this optimal level is not reached, 'recovery' from the loss may take years and be desperately unpleasant. As widows we often receive pity rather than sympathy and understanding. Pity can make bereavement worse; sympathy and understanding can be of tremendous value. Perhaps the most valuable help is having company at times when we would normally have been with our husband: watching television, going to the cinema, going shopping. The company of a friend at times such as these can often do more than drugs or visits to psychiatrists. Or you may feel like taking up some voluntary work. (See 5, Books and pamphlets).

The sense of loss, the period of mourning can last a long time – even more than a year – but when the body and mind are ready the phase passes and life becomes worth living again.

STAGES OF GRIEF AND RECOVERY

Grief can have a devastating effect. If you accept grief and if you can accept that there are three main stages of grieving you will almost certainly be able to avoid any major repercussions. If you cannot accept grief and if you grieve without the knowledge that what is happening to you is perfectly normal – nature's way of enabling us to cope – then you may find yourself physically and mentally unable to cope with life and its demands.

In the **first stage** all widows are numb. A numbness pervades everything.

Somehow this very numbness helps us to cope with what is required – arranging the funeral, coping with relatives, obtaining the death grant, applying for a pension. Although a funeral is very final many of us find the reality difficult to accept. We continue to lay a table for two, cook and shop for two, behave as if the dead person is still alive. There is nothing unusual or abnormal in this; it takes a while to adjust to being alone.

The **second stage** is the worst. This may occur anything from three days to three months after bereavement. The feeling of the emptiness of life suddenly strikes. Feelings of panic, even frenzy, are common. Feelings of guilt may predominate – 'if I'd done this he might not have died' is heard all too often. Many widows suddenly find themselves unable to remember what their husband looked like. Then there is the overriding fear of the future – 'how will I manage for money?', 'will I be able to stay in this house?', 'will I be able to pay the electricity bills?'.

This is the time when many widows withdraw – withdraw from their family, their friends and the outside world in general. It is a difficult time, a time when a fellow widow can be tremendously supportive, offering a listening ear, a shoulder to cry on and an exchange of experiences.

It is very common for widows to become **depressed** at some time after bereavement, particularly in the second stage of grieving. This is not at all surprising since the loss of a husband often means the loss of regular daily contact with others, problems of maintaining a social life, difficulties in dealing with the form filling which is a common part of life in our bureaucratized society, great concern about money, taking decisions on one's own and a considerable increase in responsibilities – particularly if there are children.

Most of us become depressed at some time in our lives but we are especially vulnerable after bereavement: whether our husband's death was unexpected or expected we are likely to become very tired, to have difficulty in sleeping, to have difficulty in maintaining a good diet (in part because the incentive to prepare meals may have gone), and these factors are not only physically debilitating but mentally debilitating too. Those of us who have had children will probably remember the intense fatigue and unexpected depression that so commonly follow childbirth; depression in widowhood can be similar but may be much more prolonged.

If you become depressed and feel that you cannot cope with life there are a number of things you can do. Try to talk to a friend or contact a member of the Widows Advisory Service. Just having someone to talk to and to rely on, even over a fairly long period of time, can be of very real help. Most of the enquiries which the National Association of Widows, and subsequently the Widows Advisory Service, receive are or have been from widows who are depressed. Almost without exception they say that it is marvellous to be able to talk with someone who understands – with someone who has gone through the same experience. Some widows find that a member of their family can help but this is rare. Perhaps this will surprise you: in our society we expect the family to support its members through difficult periods but our experience has shown family members do have great difficulty in encouraging a widow to grieve, often do not wish to talk about the death because they think that this will upset the widow and thus they may actually, unconsciously, impede the process of recovery.

For some widows medical help is necessary. A vicious circle may be set up whereby the apathy and lethargy associated with depression make matters worse: the housework does not get done, financial matters go unattended, the children become an intolerable strain...these can make one even more depressed. Therefore it is sometimes essential to go to your family doctor; s/he ought to listen to you sympathetically and may treat you directly or recommend that you see a psychiatrist. This depression may respond very well to drugs and after a short time the depression passes away; sometimes drugs are given in hospital so that you can be observed to ensure the right dosage.

Sometimes bereavement strikes during the menopause. Thus there will be physical reactions to the change in life to be coped with too. Apathy and depression often accompany the menopause and thus again it is important to seek medical advice if you feel that you cannot cope. Hormone replacement therapy is gradually becoming available in Britain and has clearly helped many American women not only to maintain their youthfulness but also to eliminate the physical and mental problems (including depression) sometimes associated with the menopause. If you would like to read about hormone replacement therapy Wendy Cooper's book *No Change* explores not only how it works but the importance of trying to persuade British family doctors to let their patients try it. *The Women's Directory* by Carolyn Faulder, Christine Jackson and Mary Lewis lists the menopause clinics in Britain.

The **third stage** may be reached from one to two years after bereavement. This is the stage when widowhood is accepted and when a new life can begin. Once this stage is reached positive planning for the future can take place. Acceptance of a new role gradually occurs and the torments of the previous months gradually fade. If you are in this third stage you will probably agree., that it is still not easy to cope with life: practical and emotional problems do not disappear completely but on the whole they are easier to deal with.

Mary Stott writes . . .

To write of how I learned to be a widow and eventually to stop thinking of myself as a widow is to risk the disapproval of some of the people whose opinion I value most. Yes, one should contain one's grief. But one of the things I have learned through all this is that we who have words can articulate grief for those who have not, and that to have grief spelt out, its pattern charted, is something we all obscurely need.

K died on 29th November, 1967. He was fifty-six. We were going through a severe family crisis which necessitated our compiling together a very difficult statement. K scribbled some notes and then said he felt unwell and had better go to bed. 'I'll finish it in the morning,' he said. 'Like hell you will,' I thought to myself, and sat down at the typewriter, running up- and down-stairs every few minutes. 'I think you had better phone the doctor,' he said, about midnight. The doctor, a locum, said what pills to give him and to ring back if necessary. I showed K what I had written and he grinned. 'I only did this to get out of doing the job,' he said. It was the last thing he said to me. Good for me that the last words were a little joke. There came that dreadful rattle in the throat and though, of course, I phoned the doctor again I suppose I knew. I lay across him and put my mouth on his, but with a feeling of helpless inefficiency. What did I know about mouth-to-mouth resuscitation? The doctor came, very tall, very dark-skinned, very uncommunicative. A stranger. He gave me, I think, a sedative, and went away. It was three o'clock in

the morning and I was alone in a very large house. I don't remember
weeping. My one thought was that somehow I must get through the
next three hours before I could communicate with the outside world.
There wasn't anyone I felt I could wake from sleep with this news,
least of all my poor daughter. It never occurrred to me that one
could phone the undertaker in the dead of night. I know now that
any woman could knock up her neighbour and get help, but all I
could think of then was that about six o'clock I could phone K's
nephew, Denys Stott, who made a very early start for work. I hope
no other woman, stuck as I was, will think she has to wait to cry for
help, even at 3 a.m. on a cold November morning. So I wandered up
and downstairs, making tea and coffee, going in and out of the
bedroom, to lay my head on K's shoulder or kiss his hands. There
was nothing frightening to me about his still warm body. He was still
my love. If I took a sedative – and I truly cannot remember – it
induced not the smallest inclination to sleep. So I settled down to
write letters to my friends. 'It was a strange letter,' one of them told
me afterwards. I expect those letters *were* strange. I can remember
writing in one, 'I feel a great life force in me.' Little I knew then that
it was only a merciful illusion.

So at 6 o'clock I phoned Denys. 'Good God,' he said, and put the
phone down. It is hard at first to realize that your friends are
shocked too; that they too cannot speak for grief. Two hours still
to go before I could venture to make the other phone calls, to our
daughter, to K's friend and editor, to my friend the northern
features editor, to Helen, my closest friend.

I scratched up the willpower to phone the undertaker and to
dictate a telegram to my brother and that was my lot. I am glad I
could cope rationally with what had to be done, but I think now
that no woman should feel she has to drive herself to get out these
dreadful words. Anyone, almost literally anyone, would do it for
you, glad to be able to serve your need. The respect and tenderness
for grief are universal, and the effect of shock is worse for many
women than it was for me. I had the strong comfort of knowing that
my husband had suffered scarcely at all (though who knows if there
is a moment of intolerable agony in the moment of the coronary
thrombosis?). I could say, 'Thank heaven you are out of it all, my
poor love'; out of the pain of the family crisis, out of the misery of
ill-health; out of the sense of the failure of his life's work at the
death of the *News Chronicle*. I was not, I found, frightened of death
itself. But many women are terrified. They need someone to take
charge and no one should hesitate to ask. They will not be refused.

So by nine o'clock help began to arrive. I found I could cope with
the undertaker because he was a plain blunt man from the Co-op
who minced no words and did not sentimentalize over me. And I
knew what documents he and the doctor needed and where they
were to be found. It was then that a strange persistent obsession with
the problems of all widows took hold of me. I pictured having to
scrabble through K's drawers, even his pockets to find the papers we
needed; I pictured having no money in hand to buy food, or even
stamps. For God's sake, I wanted to yell, don't wait until it is too

late to know where your husband keeps his essential papers; don't
ever leave yourself short of a few quid in the Post Office or the bank.
K died at the end of a month and there was £7 in his account – he
spent as he went. I was the saver. I knew, too, what he would wish
for his funeral. We had enjoyed many macabre jokes over funerals
together. 'One pew nearer the front' he used to say, and once when
he spoke the funeral oration for a friend, another journalist friend
whispered to him as he walked back down the aisle, 'Can I book you
for mine?' He outlived K. So I knew all about that, and that he
would want his friends to be able to say goodbye to him in dignity
and fellowship, and that though we were agnostics he would think it
right that this goodbye should be in a church.

On the day of K's death I wandered about clutching, for what
reason is now beyond me, a shaggy white toy poodle belonging to
my granddaughter, vaguely stroking it and holding it close. I think I
drank a great quantity of brandy, which may have dulled my wits
but certainly did not intoxicate me. My friends phoned, arranged,
did instantly everything I asked, so that I had a curious feeling of
behaving like a queen, for the first time in my life. I slipped away
often to the bedroom to be alone with K for it seemed to me then
that he was still there. But he wasn't. He was dead. His body would
disintegrate. He was a job for the undertaker. I slammed the door
tight on this thought for many weeks but there came a day when I
walked down the garden and found a bird decaying and smelling
evilly, caught in the cherry net. Then I knew what for me is the
ultimate horror of death – not that our dear ones go elsewhere or
that they cease completely to exist, but that the bodies they have
inhabited, the bodies they *were*, the bodies so precious to us, flesh
of our flesh, are corruptible. *That* is why I cannot understand how
any human being in his senses can deliberately reduce another
human being to a carcase, a lump of inevitably decaying flesh.

So the funeral went over, which I remember very well, and the
service at the crematorium, which I remember not at all, and my
friends and family came from all over the country and wrapped me
in kindness. The need, then as they say in Lancashire, is 'to pass the
time on', to get each day over, especially the rest of the day after the
funeral. Two days later I went back to work. The thing to remember
about bereavement is that one does what one must, and no one can
imagine what this may be before it happens. I, who knew very well
that the likelihood was that I would be a widow some day, had felt
quite sure that if and when it happened I would run to my good
friend Helen. In the event, I found that nothing would have dragged
me away from the home which was, so to speak, the crown of our
thirty years of happy life together. Other widows run away from
their home in horror; a few never go back. But our dear house and
garden, K's presence there, the friendship of my neighbours, proved
the only strength I had. Unlike many bereaved women I was not
afraid to go to bed alone at night – I had done that for most of the
years of our marriage. And I did not really think out whether I
had to go to work. That was the pattern of my life and it did not
occur to me to wonder whether it should be changed. There were

the letters to answer, two or three hundred of them. For a writing
woman this may have been cathartic. For others it might have been
an impossible burden, but I think that there are very few people who
are not helped a little by having the 'condolence' letters. 'They are
so hard to write', people say. 'Whatever can one say?' It doesn't
matter much what, though it is best if one can say something in
praise of the person who has died. The comfort lies in the fact that
the pile of letters indicates your grief has some importance, however
brief. You may need to go back to them again and again later when
everyone else seems to have forgotten and you yourself are more
afraid of forgetting than of remembering.

I think perhaps it is true, as people often say now, that we have
pruned away too many of our mourning rituals and expect too much
of the bereaved in behaving rationally, discreetly, courageously. No
blinds are drawn round the house of death now, as when my mother
died. The funeral cars pass unnnoticed – one of my keenest memories
of my mother's funeral is the men on either side of the road raising
their hats like puppets all the way to the crematorium. But I truly
do not know where the answer lies. To make a parade of grief, to
institutionalize its forms, as the Victorians did so grotesquely, is
perhaps even worse than to treat death as a regrettable brief incident.
I would sooner have gone to K's funeral in what I happened to have
on than make a show of myself with crepe and veil and weepers.

Grief is an illness of the psyche. To formalize opportunities for
its release, for weeping, wailing, yelling at fate is unlikely to help.
Tears don't come to order and if they did, how could they bring
relief? Rage creeps up on you unawares too. I was coming back from
London and as I walked along a crowded compartment and saw
people laughing and talking and reading and sleeping something in
my mind went briefly out of gear. Their normality was hideous to
me. I was in hostile country, an enemy alien. Fortunately two
friends were waiting for me at the end of my journey. The mental
processes slipped back into gear. It does not happen so quickly for
everyone. I used to say for myself that like Katherine Mansfield's
poor 'Ma Parker' I had no private place to cry. It wasn't true,
because I had a whole empty house to cry in – but so often the need
for tears came when I was at work, when it could not be satisfied.
The body's protest at this rigid self-discipline was the quite terrifying
exhaustion that came over me at times, so that I could barely lift
my hand from the arm of a chair. As with many another woman,
the sense of loss sometimes manifested itself in a searing physical
pain, somewhere in the guts. It might have gone more easily for
me if I had not slammed the door as tightly as I could on recollection
of what had happened – I came to think later that I had slammed it
against K as well as against anguish – but at the time there was no
question of choice. In grief we do as we must.

It seemed to me that I must not delay the sorting out of K's possessions, the giving away of his clothes. It is a brutal job of butchery
of one's integrated life with another human being, and sometimes I
moaned like an animal. Let no one think I blame any woman who
cannot or will not face it for years. I understand very well the

passionate clutching to oneself all that was 'his'. But I fortified myself with scorn for Queen Victoria who thought she could keep Albert with her by retaining round her all his things just as they were. The aura that personal possessions, especially clothes, take on from their owner, so dreadfully poignant at first, lasts a pitifully little while.

Self-pity was easy to identify as the supreme enemy – easier for me, I dare say, than for many, because as a woman's page editor, I knew more than most about the problems of widows. 'Why did it have to happen like this to me?' could not be allowed, for I knew very well that there were three million widows in this country alone, and that for many of them it must have been very much worse than for me. No doubt my obsession with their plight, their lack of money, lack of job, of experience in standing on their own feet was part of my defence mechanism. I felt driven to write about 'Learning to be a widow' in the *Guardian* and to speak of it on BBC Woman's Hour. It was thought a very courageous thing to do, but the only thing that took a little willpower was controlling my voice as I read the scripts – and how tenderly supportive was my Woman's Hour producer. Putting things into words was my habit of life, the need to identify with the Three Million, to try to help the still secure to prepare themselves just a little for the state of widowhood, was a compulsion. In grief we do as we must.

My own basic problem was not money or security or health, it was simply learning, after thirty years, to live alone. The practical things were a bit troublesome, but few were impossible. What was so hard was breaking the habit of having someone to talk to – about the day's papers, what went on at work, the meals, the garden, the state of the nation, anything that came to mind. Even during all those years when K worked by night and I by day we had talked on the telephone very frequently and unfailingly at 11 o'clock at night. Even now I find it difficult to imagine myself into the life of the happily solitary people who feel no need to talk about what they have read, seen, heard, thought, to any other person. It wasn't, with me, that there was really no one to talk to – there were colleagues, friends, neighbours, and in the early days I understood very well the need to make it easy for them to talk to *me*, to protect them against the embarrassment that they might be 'intruding on my grief' or that I might burst into tears. (Though people really should not mind risking that. It's a very small thing to bear, having a weeping woman on your hands, compared with the release it may give her.)

It was a little later that it came to me that there was no one I could talk to as of right. When you are suddenly bereft of your 'speech-friend' (as William Morris called it) you fear that by engaging in conversation with anyone else you are asking a favour. Social assurance is more precarious than we think, for it rests on the assumption that by and large it is mutually agreeable. Gauche adolescents find it impossible to believe that anyone would actually enjoy talking to them; so do people whose inner security has collapsed, through bereavement, divorce, desertion, disgrace, being made redundant or any other reason. I began to have some insight into loneliness. All those letters from widows spelling out for me their sense of isolation, of being excluded from society, made me well aware of what the poor beggars were clutching at, and that I too might clutch too hard, might expect too much of my friend. My own best help came from a friend who turned up almost every Saturday evening to play two piano duets, bringing the pudding for our supper in the boot of his car. I worried a lot lest he should think I was becoming too dependent on his friendship and on the regularity of our sessions, but clung to the thought that I was giving a little – even if only in the fairly rare boon of having two pianos – as well as taking.

Losing K made me much more passionately 'liberationist' in that it revealed to me very sharply how much greater my resources were than those of a wife who had been totally dependent on her husband, not only financially, but socially. How do they survive, these left-over halves of couples who did everything together, whose friends were all couples like themselves, who went everywhere together, had no job but looking after a home and the man who is gone? I had not only ample money and the dignity of a job, but friends of my own. They were K's friends too, but initially and permanently *my* friends. They did not slip out of my life when I became a woman on my own. My experience tallied with that of other widows in that my husband's colleagues and men friends fairly quickly drifted out of my life. It caused me some sorrow, but no bitterness. They had their own lives to lead, their own problems. Flaying myself, rather than other widows, I was scornful of women who wail that they are never invited anywhere but will not see that they can do the inviting. Cruel, really, because many of us are too broken-backed to make the effort. But the thought served me in my need and drove me to ensure that I was never entirely alone during the long hours of Saturday and Sunday.

It is true what widows say, that our society is cruel to the woman on her own. A lone woman is a complication. Widows have told me that wives regard them not only as a drag but as a threat — and it seems to be true that some men find the widow irresistibly attractive. My age, no doubt — I was sixty, four years older than K — as well as the sort of company we kept, protected me from passes by men assuming that the widow must be avid for sex.

Well, so I planned my days in what I believed to be a very rational, therapeutic way. I gave the go-ahead for the building of a carport K had planned, though the new car had been driven by a friend back to the dealer's within a few days of his death. It would improve the house; it could be let. I agreed with my dear neighbours that they should take over two rooms of our rather curiously interlocked 'semis'. This meant another painful clear out, but it made good sense. I had occasional gatherings of friends. I had a laburnum tree planted in the garden and put in bedding plants and bulbs. I was doing all the kinds of things I urge any widow to do.

And then it hit me. There wasn't any real point in doing any of this, I was hollow inside. I was less than half a person. Behind the carefully maintained facade there was nothing, or at least nothing that really mattered. I must try to explain about this phase of bereavement because only those who have been through it know about it, and it is, I am certain, about three months after the death, when many of us appear to be doing quite nicely, that the collapse of the will to live occurs. It is then that widows, and widowers too, especially if they have no dependent children, need to be taken into the care of their friends. What needs to be done is just to keep them ticking over; to ask them on little visits, giving them little jobs to do, nothing very much, nothing very demanding, just small things to fill in the emptiness of the personality as well as of the days. At this stage, Death is the friend, Life is the enemy. It seemed to me at this time that being alive was just a habit that had now become very disagreeable. Now I had been jolted out of the normal view that it is obviously better to be alive than dead, it seemed a ludicrous proposition. What was so wonderful about being alive? Sixty years of life had habituated me to eating at certain times, washing, dressing, going to work, doing this and that — but *what for?* Why spend another ten or twenty years doing all these things just for the sake of being alive? There were, it is true, fleeting moments of pleasure but there was nothing, *nothing*, that made the future look anything but a dreary, meaningless trudge. The concept of life as a duty, in the abstract, struck me as monstrous. Though duty to *people*, yes: I had a great, over-riding obligation to my daughter, and could not run away from that.

Once my angle of vision on life and death had swung round I believe I got a certain kind of bleak, cynical pleasure from contemplating the view. I was Outside, looking in; uninvolved, uncaring, detached; in a sense free. One of my widowed friends told me she threw away her bottle of sleeping pills in case they should be an irresistible temptation. I looked on mine as my greatest comfort and strength, the guarantee that at any time I could quietly decide that enough was enough. Of course that time wasn't to be yet; there was no hope of letting myself off the hook of obligation in the foreseeable future. But *some day* I could lay down my heavy load, say, 'thank you for having me,' and put myself to sleep. I was so much more than 'half in love with easeful death'. Lovely, lovely death; not necessarily an end, not necessarily a beginning. Never once did I allow myself to hope for a reunion with K, but I thought that perhaps his 'spirit' if there is such a thing — and mine, one day — might be merged into a sort of stream of consciousness.

Gardening had made me very much aware that in nature nothing ceases to exist. The 'death' of a plant means that it changes its nature, disintegrates into the soil, makes humus, fertilizes other plants. It is hard to believe that what animates a sentient being is lost when the heart ceases to beat; the beating of the heart, the inflation of the lungs are an explanation of how life is maintained, not in any sense an explanation of what life *is*. What was the impulse that *made* the heart beat, the lungs inflate. I kept asking myself; what was the impulse that enabled the brain cells to collate and transform the information transmitted to them by the senses of Beethoven's *Eroica* or Shakespeare's *Hamlet*? Why should this impulse, analogous, I thought, to electro-magnetic waves, stop short when the heart stopped beating? The unplugging of a television set does not mean that the electro-magnetic waves cease to flow, only that they cease to function at that particular point of outlet.

What drove me to explore these ideas was the sense that K's death had not only bereaved but mutilated me. Whatever he was and whatever I was had become so inextricably mingled through thirty years together that when what was K was abruptly wrenched away the machine for living that was Mary seemed to be lacking some essential parts. I thought then that the damage was permanent and I am sure that with some people it is so. My psyche proved to be stronger than I thought — indeed, than I hoped, for at this stage I bitterly resented the idea that I should be clutched back into the habit of living, that the instinctive will to live might reassert itself and that in old age I might lose the will to die, which to me would be a very shameful thing.

The time stretched out. There was the job, the family, music, the house and garden, friends. Helen invited me to join her and another friend on a crazy car trip through Rumania and Hungary. I, a non-driver, often sat broodily for long hours in the back of the car, wedged between sleeping bags and luggage but we shared much hilarity in our search for overnight accommodation. Perhaps the discovery that mourning does not preclude bellyaching laughter is a turning point. It takes a long while for the bereaved to experience conscious happiness; much longer to admit to being happy, for that seems an intolerable disloyalty. Yet the return to normality has to be at the cost of the recession of the lost one. One may say, and often does, that the bloodiest anguish is better than forgetting, but the anguish slowly, and by no means steadily, recedes too. Life creeps in unawares to restore the mutilated personality. For weeks I was a non-person; for many, many months a half person and now I have to admit — reluctantly, because it was better to be part of a dual entity — that I am at least as much a whole person as many people who have never been chopped in half. I never consciously sought to create 'a life of my own', nor indeed actively hoped for or wanted it. It just happened, gradually, by doing what I had to do, by very determinedly filling up all the hours so that I seldom mouldered away on my own, by responding civilly, even if not with enthusiasm, to whatever invitations or stimuli came my way — and by quite savagely rejecting the idea that the widow should be a life-long object of pity or, indeed, is more to be pitied than many other people who have suffered cruel loss or rejection, or who have never enjoyed the fullness of life. I know that if the mutilated personality is to survive it cannot be by trying to keep the Other alive, by emotional self-indulgence; it can only be by letting the habit of living take over until one can respond again to what life has to offer. As it gradually took over for me.

I had one more hurdle to surmount. The house; the garden. In the summer of 1969 Helen and I spent a month in America. I got home very early on a beautiful, sunny July morning to find a notice on the door. 'Welcome to Home Sweet Home. We're all here' — perhaps the sweetest, most heart-warming thing my daughter ever did for me, and I drifted round the garden cutting off the dead rose heads, very much in love with its healing beauty, until it seemed

time to make a pot of tea for μs all. But from that time the thought
began to take shape, 'What am I doing, maintaining this large house,
this very large garden, just for me?'

That I could begin, very gingerly at first, to explore the idea of
moving was an indication of how far I had moved, in less than two
years, along the road to being a separate entity again, for it was
probably in our attachment to this house and garden that we had
been most closely integrated. We had lived there nearly twenty
years. If I went, I left most of my life with K behind. My only child
lived in London and I was within sight of retirement, when I could
need contact with her and her family more than ever. If I stayed, I
had evidences of K's presence all about me — but they must have
been fading a little, or how could I have even begun to think of
pulling up the roots that spread so deep and wide? So it is for many
of us — within two years we become able to act rationally, no longer
instinctively. Reason said 'Go', and having established with the
editor of the *Guardian* that my move to the London office would
not be unwelcome, I set about the next bloody, brutal surgical
operation, by putting the house up for sale. I am glad now, though I
was very disconcerted then, that a firm offer for it came within days,
for it forced me into action — into finding a flat in Blackheath,
reasonably near to my daughter. Of course it was all sickeningly
painful. How could it be otherwise? Yet working out with pencil,
paper, ruler, measuring tape, which carpets, which furniture would
fit where and hold what, was an interesting and therapeutic exercise.
All intellectual exercises are therapeutic once the wits have begun to
function again.

So in February, 1970 I came to London and after the inevitably
miserable, frustrating, lonely weeks of settling into the flat, what I
had thought to be a decaying plant's feeble suckers proved to be
viable new growth. A person began to emerge who might not have
been able, or wished, to emerge had our joint life continued. Now I
am alone I am free. Sometimes I am very lonely, and more painfully
so when there is some small triumph or success and no one to rejoice
with me, than in trouble or disappointment. But freedom has its
compensations — freedom to come and go, freedom to do the things
one refrained from doing before, freedom to explore new patterns
of life; freedom, if one has a mind to it, to become an elderly
eccentric.

Elderly. That is a thought I should take into my mind now I am
in my mid-sixties and retired from full-time work. Elderly. How
absurd. I no longer run for buses or upstairs, but I chase small
Charlotte round the garden or up and down the corridor. I am not
deceiving myself about the quality of my life. It is quite rich; quite
enviable. I do not need to wonder yet, I think, how long I have left
to enjoy the mental and physical pleasures of being alive.

Shall I put away then for a while the thought that the body will
inevitably deteriorate and the mind with it? I think I safely can, for I
still feel no shrinking from the thought of death. Alex Comfort,
reviewing Simone de Beauvoir's *Old Age* in March, 1972, wrote of
death, to my surprise and dismay, as 'an irreconcilable enemy' to

which the 'natural reaction is outrage and resentment'; as 'the final dissolution, as Gerontius said, "of all that makes me Man" '. But I think that death may not be the final dissolution, and that it is not the quenching of the tiny spark of 'life' that animates the body that is outrageous but that the dissolution should be slow, humiliating, poverty-stricken, lonely. So let the politicians concern themselves that old age should not be feared because of poverty, as it was feared when it meant the workhouse; let the doctors concern themselves with removing the fear of progressive diseases which slowly paralyze the mental and physical faculties, and not with frantic efforts to fan that little spark in a hopelessly malfunctioning body. And let not the gerontologists bemuse us with the thought that the span of life must be stretched further and further and further because it is obviously better to be alive than dead. There are far too many old people cluttering up the earth now and if we were not so afraid of death we should be able to see that to deny life to the unborn while determinedly prolonging the life of the worn-out old is a very strange illogicality.

Why are we so afraid to be dead? We are no longer afraid of hell-fire. Is it that we have been deprived of the hope of heaven? Isn't sweet oblivion enough? Perhaps one day physicists exploring the ultimate constituents of the universe, energy and mass, particle and wave, and the parapsychologists exploring the strange phenomena of thought and 'mind' may join together to provide us with a substitute for heaven, some meaning and purpose in Life beyond what we can now grasp while we totter around on our two uncertain legs in the space-time continuum. Something to look forward to?

As for me, it is because death is still the friend that life has ceased to be the enemy. Whatever happens, hopefully when *I* choose, there will be an end. And perhaps a beginning.

This extract is taken from Mary Stott's book *Forgetting's No Excuse* (Virago 1975), and is reproduced here by kind permission of Faber & Faber Ltd.

Most of us have little idea of what to do when someone dies. It is something we experience more frequently as we get older but often for the widow it is her husband's death which is the first one with which she has to deal. Many of the things to be done can be done either by you or a relative or friend. Indeed, relatives and friends will *want* to help you.

If your husband has died in *hospital* the doctor in charge will issue a **Certificate of Death.** The hospital may want to carry out a post mortem but this cannot be done without your consent. If you wish the body to be cremated the hospital will arrange for you to be given all the necessary forms and the doctor will arrange for another doctor to examine the body (there must be two doctors' signatures on the form for cremation).

If your husband has died at *home* then you must call a doctor. If the death has been unexpected or violent then you should not touch anything until the doctor has been. The doctor will issue a Certificate of Death. If you wish the body to be cremated you should tell the doctor so that he can arrange for a second doctor to sign the certificate. You will then have to contact an undertaker (or funeral director as he is normally called) who will come and take the body to a Chapel of Rest where it will stay until the funeral or cremation.

The death must be registered at the office of the Registrar of Births, Marriages and Deaths in whose area the death has occurred. Normally the person to do this is you, the widow; but if you feel that you cannot do it then a near relation or friend can do it for you. The Registrar will need to know details of your husband's age and occupation, and the age of next of kin. He will enter these details and the details on the Certificate of Death into the Register. You, or the person registering the death, will then have to sign the Register with the Registrar's own pen. A death should be registered within five days in England and Wales and within eight days in Scotland.

The Registrar will then give you a copy of the entry, a disposal certificate (which means that you can proceed with the funeral arrangements), and one free copy of the Certificate of Registration of Death, Form BD 8. The Certificate of Registration of Death is an important form; you will need a copy of it in order to claim national insurance benefits, to make claims on life insurance policies; you will need one when settling your husband's estate. Currently the charge is £1.25 for each extra copy and you can have as many copies as you wish. If at a later stage you need an extra copy you can go back to or write to the registrar.

If there is to be an **inquest** you cannot, of course, register the death. But you can ask the Coroner to issue a written statement which can be used instead of a Certificate of Registration of Death in order to claim national insurance benefits (eg. widow's allowance) or supplementary benefits.

When you have obtained the certificate of disposal you can go ahead and make **arrangements for either burial or apply for cremation**. If you want cremation you must complete four additional forms – an application for cremation on Form A and certificates from three different doctors on forms B, C and F. Forms B and C are known as the 'cremation certificates' and doctors usually charge £5.50 for completing each of them. The final form is completed by the medical referee of the crematorium and his fee of £2 is usually included in the crematorium's basic charge. Today most people prefer cremation.

Once you have obtained the relevant certificates you can either arrange the funeral yourself or employ a funeral director. Most people use the services of a funeral director.

Funeral directors do not work to office hours: you can call on them at any time. However, extra charges may be made for some services if these are done outside normal working hours – services such as removal of the body. Funeral directors will make all the arrangements for you, including contacting the vicar, church,crematorium etc according to your needs.

If you do decide to use a funeral director you should contact him as soon as possible. It is always worth approaching at least two firms because the service offered varies and so do the charges. It is also important to ask for a written estimate of charges. Many firms of funeral directors have a printed price list or a brochure but even so it is easy to underestimate the actual final costs. Funerals usually are more expensive than people expect.

In 1976 the average charge for a funeral was about £165 for cremation and £180 for burial. These charges included a veneered chipboard coffin, a hearse, one car for the mourners, bearers, doctors' cremation certificates, crematorium or graveyard charges, church fees, and the funeral director's supervision and attendance. The cost of the main items is made up in the following way: about £50 for the coffin, £13 for the hearse, £11 for the mourners' car, £11 for cremation certificates, £23 for the crematorium or £43 for the cemetery charges and about £10 in church fees. These costs reflect a very simple and cheap funeral.

Examples of the costs of extra items are as follows: a more elaborate coffin about £30, an ordinary wreath £7, embalming £10, additional cars about £12 each; the funeral director will also arrange flowers but may charge up to about 25 per cent commission. Thus you will see that most funerals cost at least £200.

You may want also to have a memorial. A simple entry in a Book of Remembrance may cost anything from £2 to £15; the fee for a memorial rose bush may be anything from £5 to £50; a simple headstone may cost between £70 and £100 and a slightly more elaborate headstone may cost up to £300. (These figures have been taken from the report of the Price Commission of *Funeral Charges*, HMSO, 1977.)

Therefore you can see that it is worth trying to talk to more than one funeral director to get a clear idea of how he arranges his services, whether he embalms, and what his charges will be. Obviously it is not easy to be 'businesslike' when arranging a funeral and you may ask a relation or friend to deal with it for you. Whether you arrange it yourself or ask someone else to do it for you, insist that the funeral director itemizes all charges individually on the invoice so that you can check through afterwards.

Most funeral directors will not demand payment immediately. They appreciate that bereavement is stressful and that financial matters can take some weeks to be sorted out. However **on receiving the bill** you should check through the details of charges carefully. If you have difficulty in meeting the overall cost then you should ask the funeral director to allow you to pay in instalments.

Your husband may have taken out an insurance policy to cover the cost of his funeral. If you think that this is so then look through his papers and, if necessary, see his solicitor and/or bank manager if they hold any of his documents. Your solicitor may advise you on meeting the funeral costs.

If there is no insurance policy and if you are very short of money you can approach the Department of Health and Social Security (DHSS) for a grant or a loan. You will probably be entitled to receive a Death Grant (normally of

£30) and you may be able to get an extra grant to cover the cost of the 'basic' funeral. Entitlement to receive a Death Grant depends upon national insurance contributions and you apply to the national insurance section of the DHSS;. entitlement to an additional grant or loan depends entirely upon your resources and you apply to the supplementary benefits section of the DHSS. (see the next section on Money for Immediate Needs).

MONEY FOR IMMEDIATE NEEDS

You may be entitled to receive a **death grant.** This is a small sum of money designed to help you to meet the costs incurred at the time of death. A claim for a death grant can be made on the basis either of your husband's own national insurance contributions or on your contributions – if you have been paying full contributions into the national insurance scheme.

If your husband was born between 5 July 1883 and 5 July 1893 you will receive a death grant of £15; if your husband was born on or after 5 July 1893 you will receive £30.

If your husband left a will, or Letters of Administration have been taken out, the grant normally will be paid to the executors or administrators (see section on Wills and Intestacy).

To claim the death grant you need to complete the back of the certificate given to you by the Registrar and to complete the application form for a death grant which you may obtain either from the Registrar or from your local office of the DHSS.

The form on which you apply for the death grant asks a number of straight-forward questions; however it is quite likely that at the time of completing the form you will not have all of the required information to hand and you must simply indicate 'don't know' or 'I will send this on later'. *Do not delay* submitting the form for lack of information. You must submit your claim for a death grant within six months of your husband's death. If you submit your application later than this you must show what is known as 'good cause'; for example, a late claim would be accepted if your husband had been missing for a long period and his death had not been established until much later.

Further details about Death Grants are given in the leaflet NI 49 Death Grant which you can obtain from your local office of the Department of Health and Social Security. Staff at the DHSS office will be pleased to help you to complete the form, especially if you are in doubt because you do not have all of the information being requested.

You may be entitled to claim a **widow's allowance**. This depends upon your husband's national insurance contribution record and fuller details are given in section 3. Widow's allowance is a national insurance benefit paid for 26 weeks to help you to adjust to your new financial circumstances. The amount that you will receive depends upon not only your husband's national insurance contribution record but also on whether you have dependent children. From November 1977 the basic weekly rate for a widow without children was £24.50.

It is important that you apply for your widow's allowance as soon as possible by writing or going to your local office of the Department of Health and Social Security. Sometimes it takes up to three weeks for widow's allowance to start to be paid (backdated to the time of the beginning of widowhood) because the records have to be checked.

If you do find yourself in urgent need of cash then you can apply for **supplementary benefit** at your local office of the Department of Health and

Social Security. Again, fuller details of how to do this are given in Section 3. Supplementary benefit is available to any person whose income is temporarily or over a long period of time inadequate for their needs. Thus even though you may be entitled to widow's allowance you may find that supplementary benefit can tide you over until the allowance comes through. Supplementary benefit can be paid immediately either on a weekly basis or exceptionally in the form of a grant or loan.

If you are temporarily short of cash you should ask your local council or landlord to wait awhile for payment of rent; explain that your husband has died and that your financial position is being sorted out. If you apply for and get supplementary benefit then you will receive an amount to cover your rent. If you are not receiving supplementary benefit you should talk to a member of staff of your local council to see whether you should apply for a rent rebate or allowance. Both council and private tenants can apply for rent rebates. The amount of a rent rebate or rent allowance depends upon your income and other resources and will change accordingly.

You may already have been receiving a **rate** rebate. If so you should notify your local council of your bereavement so that your rebate can be adjusted (normally it will be increased) promptly. If you are not already receiving a rate rebate then you should enquire about whether you are likely to become eligible and if so apply immediately.

If your rate demand has just come in or comes while your finances are being sorted out then explain your new circumstances to your local council and if necessary ask for a delay in payment until your financial position is clear.

If you are an *owner occupier* with a **mortgage** you should approach the Building Society as soon as possible. Explain that your husband has died and that you are finding out whether there is a mortgage protection policy. If there is such a policy then the insurance company will pay the balance outstanding on the mortgage and you will have no further mortgage commitments to make – the house will be yours. If there is no mortgage protection policy then you will assume responsibility for mortgage repayments on the amount still outstanding. Many widows find this a frightening prospect and become very worried that they will lose their family home. You should not worry. If there continues to be a mortgage commitment you may find that you can claim supplementary benefit or you may be able to earn enough to enable you to keep up the commitment. What is most important in the short run is that you see the manager of the Building Society (or the mortgage may be with an insurance company or local authority) and explain that your financial affairs are being sorted out. Ask him, in the meantime, to bear with you and to allow you to repay just the interest element of the mortgage; you will probably find that a large part of the monthly repayments your husband was making was repayment of capital rather than interest. For all policies, except insurance linked endowment schemes, it will in general be true to say that the longer you have had the mortgage the larger the amount of repayment taken up with capital rather than interest.

OTHER THINGS TO BE DONE AS SOON AS POSSIBLE

Whether you rent or own your home you should get the **tenancy** or ownership transferred into your own name as soon as possible. If you are using a solicitor you can talk to him about this. If you are not using a solicitor then approach your local Citizens' Advice Bureau (CAB) for guidance.

Inform both your own (if you work) and your husband's **tax office** that he has died. Do this as quickly as possible in order to avoid problems in the future. Whether or not you work your tax code will have to be adjusted to take account of your new circumstances and delays can result in large tax demands anything from six months to three years after the beginning of widowhood. Widow's allowance is taxable and many widows do not realize this, particuarly if they have not been working.

When you inform the tax office(s) about your husband's death you should do so in writing and try to keep a copy of your letter. If you keep copies of correspondence it is easier to sort out any problems which may arise later. If you are unsure about the address of your husband's tax office you should look in the local telephone directory and contact the offices listed under 'H.M. Inspector of Taxes'. The relevant office will be the one nearest your husband's place of work rather than your home.

It is almost always necessary to contact a **solicitor** when someone dies. This applies regardless of whether your husband left a will. If you have a low income then you will be able to receive advice on legal matters either free of charge or for a small sum. Further details are given in Section 3.

3 After the funeral

WILLS, PROBATE AND INTESTACY

Wills

When a man dies, the executors of his will have the duty to dispose of his body and the right to decide, within certain limits how to dispose of it. Where there are no executors anyone may take responsibility for disposing of the body and the local authority must do so if it appears that no suitable arrangements have been made.

Your husband may have specified in his will the way he wanted his body to be disposed of. He may have wanted to be buried in a particular plot or he may have specified cremation. He may have requested that his body be used for medical research or that parts of his body be used for transplant operations.

For the most part any such wishes are not legally binding. However, your husband's body may not be used for medical purposes if he has expressed an objection before death or if you object after his death. It may therefore be important to look for the will as soon as possible after death if you want to respect your husband's wishes. Prompt action may be essential, especially where the body is to be used for medical research.

If you do not know where to find the will, ask your husband's solicitor and his bank. The solicitor may well have a copy, even if he does not have the original, and this may give you the information you need.

Probate

If your husband has left a will it should make it much easier to settle his affairs. It will normally name two executors, of whom you may be one and perhaps his solicitor or the bank the other, whose duty it will be to administer his estate. This means that his executors must gather his assets, pay his debts and taxes, and distribute what is left in accordance with the will.

It is usual, although not always essential, for executors to apply for a grant of probate. When the court grants probate it means that the will is valid and that the executors are validly appointed. Probate is usually necessary because some assets will only be handed over to the executors on production of probate. Probate is not needed to obtain payment of various kinds of assets where the sums involved are less than £1,500. These sums include wages and pensions due to servicemen, civil servants and local authority employees. Many other employers adopt a similar policy.

Many kinds of national savings are payable without probate, as are deposits in the Trustee Savings Bank, the National Savings Bank (the Post Office), Building Societies and Social Security benefits.

Probate is obtained from the probate registry or, where the net value of the estate is less than £2,000, from the county court. There is a district probate registry in most large towns. You may apply for probate yourself or you may employ a solicitor to do so. His fees will be a debt of the estate and therefore payable before anything is distributed to the beneficiaries.

It often takes a year or more to wind up an estate. One of the reasons for this is that the executors have to account to the Inland Revenue in case any capital transfer tax is payable. Valuing assets can take time and there may be disputes with the Inland Revenue over the accuracy of valuations. No tax is usually payable where the estate is worth less than £15,000. If the estate is taking a long time to settle, it may be possible to make interim payments on account to the major beneficiaries. If a solicitor is administering the estate you should not hesitate to ask him to do this. He should be able to estimate the tax that will be payable with a reasonable degree of accuracy.

It will obviously take longer to settle an estate if the will is contested. The will may be contested even though probate has already been granted. If you wish to contest a will, or if your husband's will is contested by someone else, you should consult a solicitor.

The main grounds are that a will was not properly executed, that the testator was not of sound mind, that the will lacked his knowledge and approval, or that it was obtained by undue influence or by fraud.

Intestacy

If your husband has died without leaving a will, there are rules to decide who should administer his estate and how it should be distributed.

As his widow, you have the first claim to administer your husband's estate. To do so formally you will need to apply for letters of administration, which have the same effect as a grant of probate. But it will not be necessary to do this in circumstances where it would not be necessary to apply for probate. So if your husband has left no houses or land but has deposited £1,000 in the Trustee Savings Bank you should not need to apply for letters of administration.

The rules which govern how your husband's estate will be distributed are rather complicated, and only a summary can be given here. They are based on a survey of the provisions in a large number of wills in the early part of this century and are therefore designed to reflect the 'average' will.

How much you will inherit will depend on two things: the size of the estate and the claims of other relatives. But there are two situations where you will inherit the whole estate. The first is where your husband has no children or other close relatives who survive him. No matter how large his estate may be, you will be entitled to all of it (after tax).

The second situation is where your husband's estate is less than £25,000. Nobody else will have a claim. You also always inherit the 'personal chattels' however much they may be worth. They include cars, domestic furniture, pictures, ornaments, jewellery, musical instruments, wine and consumable stores but only if they were not used for business purposes.

If your husband leaves children or grandchildren (the children may be illegitimate) and his estate is worth more than £25,000, the distribution will be different. You will get the personal chattels, the first £25,000 (clear of tax) of the rest of the estate, and a life interest in half of what is left. If your husband leaves neither children nor grandchildren but does leave other close relatives, you will get the personal chattels, and up to £55,000 (clear of tax) from what is left of the estate. If there is anything else remaining, you will get half of it.

The figures of £25,000 and £55,000 are varied from time to time by Government order. They were increased to their present level in 1977. Your share of the estate takes priority over the claims of other relatives, even children. Of course there will often not be enough to pay even your share in full. In that case the children or grandchildren or other relatives will get nothing. Their claim is only on what is left after you have been given the capital sum and the personal chattels.

If you wish, you may take the matrimonial home in full or part satisfaction of your share of the estate. To do this you must have had your home there at the date of your husband's death. You have twelve months from the date of death to exercise this option. In that time the administrators cannot sell the house without your written consent except by order of the court or to meet debts of the estate which cannot otherwise be satisfied. This right only applies where your husband owned the house. If you owned it in joint names with him then the house will become yours in any event as his share in it will be extinguished by his death. If your husband was a tenant protected by the Rent Act then his tenancy passes to you as long as you continue to live in the house.

Family Provision

The rules set out above are not necessarily final. Whatever the will may say or whatever the effect of the intestacy rules, certain people may apply to the court for financial provision from your husband's estate. They may do so on the ground that the disposition of the estate does not make reasonable financial provision for them. The people who may do this include yourself; a former wife of your husband who has not remarried; a child of your husband (including an illegitimate child); and anyone who was being maintained by your husband.

Thus, if your husband's will leaves you out, you can apply for financial provision; but if he supported a mistress and left no will she could apply. Application must be made to the court within six months of probate or Letters of Administration being obtained. The court can order the payment of a lump sum or periodical payments.

In reaching its decision the court must consider the needs of the applicant, the needs of the beneficiaries, the obligations of your husband towards the applicant and towards the beneficiaries: the size of the estate; any disability of the applicant or the beneficiaries and the conduct of the applicant.

If you are applying, the court will consider your age, the length of the marriage and the contribution which you made to the welfare of the family. The court will bear in mind what provision you would have received if instead of his dying there had been a divorce. The court will also consider any reasons given by your husband for not making provision for you.

LEGAL AID AND SOLICITORS

It is quite possible that you will need the help of a solicitor after your husband's death. For some kinds of work you may be able to get legal aid or legal advice and assistance without charge or at a reduced rate.

Legal aid means the services of a solicitor (and a barrister if necessary) to fight a case in court. Legal advice and assistance means the services of a solicitor (and a barrister if necessary) to advise and assist you in matters which do not involve going to court. Both kinds of help are means tested, and you do not have to be very rich to find that you will have to pay for your solicitor without any help from the state. If you are on supplementary benefit or in receipt of Family Income Supplement then legal aid and legal advice and assistance will almost certainly be available without charge.

If you use a solicitor to obtain probate or Letters of Administration then you are unlikely to obtain legal advice and assistance. If the estate is small, it will not be worth using a solicitor; if there is enough in the estate to justify the use of a solicitor then legal advice and assistance is unlikely to be available. Legal aid is only available for contested cases and you may find that the costs of the case have to be paid out of what the court awards you.

If you decide to make a will yourself you should consult a solicitor. Lawyers make more money from disputes over home-made wills than they do from obtaining probate for wills they have drafted themselves. In fact, solicitors charges for drafting simple wills are very low–in the region of £10–£20. –and legal advice and assistance is available for those who cannot afford that.

You may feel that the circumstances of your husband's death entitle you to compensation. You must consult a solicitor to see if you have a claim. If your husband was a union member, and died as the result of an injury or disease contracted at work, the union may instruct its solicitor to act for you. Be sure to seek advice early: there is only a limited time in which to bring an action for damages.

WIDOWS' AND OTHER SOCIAL SECURITY BENEFITS

Successive governments have tried to make arrangements so that women who are left without the support of a man can have an income of their own. Over time these arrangements have gradually been improved so that most widows now receive some weekly benefit as of right. The arrangements are not particularly generous but they represent a vast improvement on the position for women, say, thirty years ago. Widows' benefits and most other social security benefits are increased each year. You can check current rates in leaflets NI 196 *Social Security benefit rates* available from your local social security office, referred to as the Department of Health and Social Security (DHSS).

Widows who are bereaved at the age of sixty or over or whose husband was drawing his retirement pension when he died are covered by the retirement pension scheme and the supplementary pension scheme. Widows who are bereaved under the age of sixty, or whose husband was not drawing a retirement pension when he died, are usually entitled to receive widow's allowance during the first 26 weeks of bereavement and either widow's pension or widowed mother's allowance after that until pensionable age is reached (sixty). Widows who have children are also usually able to receive increases of benefit to help support the children. Widows, with or without children, may also draw a supplementary benefit if needs exceed the weekly rate of widow's benefit or if there is no entitlement to widow's benefit.

If you were divorced or your marriage was annulled then you are not entitled to draw widow's benefit based upon your former husband's national insurance contributions. If you have not remarried and you have a child in your family towards whose maintenance your husband was liable to contribute then you may be entitled to a child's special allowance. If you were separated at the time of his death then you will be entitled to claim benefits, provided the contribution conditions referred to later were met by your husband.

Widows' Benefits

Widow's allowance is paid as a 'resettlement' benefit for the first 26 weeks of widowhood if you were under 60 when your husband died *or* he was not drawing a retirement pension, *and* provided his national insurance contributions satisfy the conditions for entitlement. If neither condition is satisfied then you will not be entitled to receive widow's allowance.

Widow's allowance is paid at a more generous rate than most other benefits. From November 1977 it was £24.50 a week. If you are a widowed mother with dependent children then you will also be entitled to claim increases of benefit for them. You may also qualify for an *earnings-related addition* to your widow's allowance. The leaflet NI 155A, obtainable from your local DHSS office explains how entitlement to earnings-related additions is calculated.

A widow who has children will normally receive **widowed mother's allowance** after the first 26 weeks of widowhood. To be entitled you must *either*
   - have one or more children under the age of 19 still living with you; *or*
   - be expecting a child by your late husband;
and your husband's national insurance contributions record must satisfy the relevant conditions.

The personal rate of benefit is lower than the rate paid during the first 26 weeks of widowhood; from November 1977 it was £17.50 a week. There is no earnings-related addition to widowed mother's allowance but you continue to receive increases for children.

You may be entitled to a **widow's pension** *either*
   - after your entitlement to widow's allowance ends if you do not qualify for widowed mother's allowance and you were over 40 when your husband died; *or*
   - if after your entitlement to widowed mother's allowance ceases you are 40 or over;
and your husband's national insurance contributions record satisfies the conditions.

The *standard rate* of widow's pension is the same as the personal rate included in the widowed mother's allowance (ie. lower than the rate paid during the first 26 weeks of widowhood); from November 1977 it was £17.50 a week. For entitlement to the standard rate of widow's pension you must have been over 50 when your husband died or when your entitlement to widowed mother's allowance ceased.

If you were between 40 and 50 when your husband died or when your entitlement to widowed mother's allowance ceased then you will receive an **age-related widow's pension**; from November 1977 the age-related widow's pension was £5.25 for a widow aged 40 when her husband died or when her entitlement to widowed mother's allowance ended; the allowance for a widow aged 49 was £16.28 a week. The amount of an age-related pension is determined by a scale – the younger the widow the lower the pension. A widow under 40 when her husband dies or when her entitlement to widowed mother's allowance ends is not entitled to any widow's pension at all.

The **contribution conditions** for giving you entitlement to benefits are explained in leaflet NI 13 – obtainable from your local office of the Department of Health and Social Security: the DHSS check your husband's contribution record and inform you accordingly of your entitlement to benefit.

If you are refused benefit or it you are awarded a weekly amount at less than the standard rate and if you feel that the DHSS has made a mistake you can **appeal** to a local national insurance tribunal. Often when a decision is challenged, if a mistake has been made, there will in fact be no appeal hearing because the matter will be corrected immediately by the DHSS. Section 4 describes how to appeal and what happens at and after an appeal.

If your husband's death was due to an **industrial accident or disease**, you may be entitled to industrial death benefit. Full details of this scheme are in leaflet NI 10 which is available from your local office of the Department of Health and Social Security.

If at the time of making your claim for widow's benefits you know that the cause of death was due to an industrial accident or a prescribed disease then you answer 'yes' to the question about this on the BW1 form. You should also send the full death certificate issued by the registrar because this states the cause of death.

Sometimes attributing a death to an industrial accident or a 'prescribed industrial disease' may be thought of long after the death. If you think that your husband's death may have been attributable in this way it is 'never too late' to claim. Each year new prescribed industrial diseases are added to the list; sometimes evidence about an industrial accident arises long after the event. If in doubt it is worth taking the necessary steps to raise the question at your local DHSS office. The level of benefit is higher than the standard widow's pension: there are no special contribution conditions.

Increases for Children

You qualify for an increase of your widow's allowance or widowed mother's allowance if you are entitled to receive child benefit for the child or children *and* the child is your own or your late husband's *or* when he died your late husband was entitled to child benefit for the child or children. (Child benefit is normally payable if you are responsible for a child under 16 or a child under 19 who is still attending school, college or university full time.) From November 1977 the increases for children were payable at a weekly rate of £7.40 for the first child and £6.90 for the second and subsequent children.

Claims for Widows' Benefits

If you are over 60 and have been getting a retirement pension on your husband's contributions you simply have to notify the DHSS of your husband's death so that your pension can be increased accordingly. You will find details of how to do this in your pension book or in the notes for guidance if you are paid four-weekly or quarterly.

If you are under sixty or if you wish to claim a widow's pension under the industrial injuries scheme (even if you are over sixty) you should complete form BW1. You can obtain this form either by applying for it on form BD8 (the Certificate of Registration of Death) or by going to your local DHSS office. Although form BW1 may look large and forbidding it is, in fact, quite easy to complete.

It is quite likely that at the time of completing the form you will not have all of the required information and documents to hand and where relevant you should simply indicate 'don't know' or 'I will send this on later'. *DO NOT DELAY* in submitting the form for lack of information or documents. Also do note that the staff of the DHSS office will be pleased to help you complete the form, especially if you are in doubt because you do not have all of the information being requested.

You must submit your claim within three months of your husband's death. If you submit your application later than this you must show what is known as 'good cause' for a late claim; for example if your husband had been missing for a long period and his death was not established until later the DHSS would, of course, accept what would technically be a late claim. Your entitlement to benefit starts not from the day you claim but from the day you became widowed.

Child's Special Allowance

If your marriage was dissolved or annulled and you have not remarried you may be entitled to claim a special allowance to help maintain any child or children in your care, towards whose maintenance your former husband contributed at least 25p a week. The allowance is based upon your deceased husband's national insurance contribution record. If awarded, you will receive the same amount per child as other widows receive in respect of their children: from November 1977 this amount was £7.40 for the first child and £6.90 for the second and subsequent children. (In addition to this amount you will already be receiving Child Benefit for the child or children.) As with other widow's benefits you must apply for Child's Special Allowance within three months of your former husband's death. If, for any reason, you have not realized that you can claim this allowance until after the three month period then it will be worth putting in a late claim and explaining the reasons for the delay. For example, you may not have found out about your husband's death until some time later; this would be regarded as 'good cause' for putting in a late claim for Child's Special Allowance. You make your claim by applying to the local office of the Department of Health and Social Security.

Further information about the Child's Special Allowance is given in leaflet NI 93 which you can obtain from the local DHSS office.

Non-contributory Pension

If your husband was over 65 on 5 July 1948 you will not be entitled to any of the above benefits because your husband would have not been able to meet the national insurance contributions conditions. If you were 40 or over when your husband died you may qualify for a non-contributory widow's pension. The standard rate if you were aged 50 or over when widowed was £10.50 in November 1977; if you were between 40 and 50 when your husband died you would receive an age-related pension which would be less than the standard rate, depending upon your age when your husband died.

Widows Who are 60 or Over

If you were 60 or over when your husband died and he had been drawing a retirement pension you can ask at the DHSS for your retirement pension to be changed to the rate for a widow if this is higher. You will also be entitled to an additional amount if your husband delayed his retirement until after he was 65. You will also receive half of his graduated pension.

If you are already drawing a retirement pension based on your own contributions, but a pension based upon your husband's contributions would be higher, then your pension can be replaced by one based on his.

If you have dependent children you can claim increases for them.

War Widow's Pensions

If your husband was, or ever had been, in the armed forces and his death could be attributed to his military service then you may be entitled to a war widow's pension. If you think that you may have a claim, write to the DHSS, Norcross, Blackpool FY5 3TA giving details of your husband's service and the circumstances of his death (ie. the reasons why you think his death is related to his service).

From November 1977 the weekly rate of pension for a war widow was £22.70 (compared with the ordinary national insurance widow's pension of £17.50 a week). Additional amounts are payable in respect of dependents and other special allowances. Further details are given in leaflet MPL 151 which you can obtain from the above address.

Methods of Payment

If you qualify for benefit you will normally receive a book of weekly orders which you can cash at a post office of your choice. Each order is valid for three months and you should try to ensure that you cash it within that time;

if you do not cash an order within three months then you can apply for a replacement order. If you fail to cash an order within twelve months of the date stated on it you will lose entitlement to cash it.

If you are entitled to a widowed mother's allowance or a pension you can choose to be paid monthly or quarterly instead. However, such payments are made 'in arrears' and in times of inflation there appears to be no advantage in choosing these methods. But if you do find this more convenient then you have to complete the application form in the national insurance leaflet NI 105 (obtainable from any local office of the Department of Health and Social Security). You will then receive your benefit in the form of crossed orders, valid for three months and payable into a bank.

Sickness, and Disablement Benefits

Payment of national insurance contributions during periods of employment may entitle you to benefits when sick or disabled. But many widows find that, even though they have paid full contributions over a long period of time, they are not eligible because of the 'overlapping benefits' rule (See Section 4 on Appeals). The overlapping benefits rule allows payment of the higher of two benefits to which a person is entitled but prevents payment of one benefit in addition to another. Thus widows who are in receipt of the full rate of widow's allowance, widow's pension or widowed mother's allowance may find that they cannot draw an additional benefit when sick or disabled.

It is important to note that sickness and industrial injury benefits are tax free and attract an 'earnings related supplement.' Therefore, if you are entitled it is very important that you check whether you will be *better off* by surrendering your widow's benefit during periods of incapacity for work.

Widow's who are in receipt of reduced rate or age-related benefits and widows who receive no widow's benefit are certain to be eligible for sickness and industrial injury benefits if enough national insurance contributions have been made (payment of the 'married woman's stamp' is sufficient for the industrial injuries scheme).

Details of the contribution conditions and how these affect the amount of benefit are given in the free leaflets listed below and obtainable from your local social security office:

NI 16 Sickness benefit

NI 5 Injury benefit for accidents at work

Leaflet NI 155A explains the earnings-related scheme.

Sickness and industrial injury benefits are paid after the first three days of incapacity for work for six months. To claim you should get a 'sick note' from your doctor and send it to your local social security office within six days of becoming incapable for work: if you have had an industrial accident or develop a disease which you think has been caused by the nature of your work then you should tell your employer and indicate the details on the same form used for applying for sickness benefit.

In November 1977 sickness benefit was payable at a weekly rate of £14.70 and industrial injury benefit at a weekly rate of £17.45. Earnings-related supplements can be paid in addition to sickness and industrial injury benefit for six months – the amount being dependent upon your earnings in the previous tax year.

Invalidity and industrial disablement benefits are also tax free and replace respectively sickness and industrial injury benefits (ie. after six months of incapacity for work). In November 1977 the standard weekly rate of invalidity pension was £17.50: invalidity allowance is paid in addition to the pension to those who becomes chronically sick under the age of 55. Industrial disablement pensions are payable (even if you return to work) at rates which vary according to the degree of disablement, assessed by a medical board: pensions can be increased with special hardship allowances, unemployability supplements, constant attendance allowances, exceptionally severe disablement allowances and hospital treatment allowances. Sickness or invalidity benefit can be paid in addition to disablement benefit unless an unemployability supplement is also being paid.

Leaflet NI 16A describes the invalidity benefit scheme and leaflets NI 2, NI 3, NI 6 and NI 207 describe the industrial disablement scheme.

The **Non-contributory invalidity pension** scheme is for people of working age who have been continuously incapable of work for 6 months and who do not qualify for any of the sickness or disablement benefits which are based on contributions. To be entitled you must be under 60 and benefit is affected by receipt of widow's benefits. Leaflet NI 210 describes the scheme and includes a claim form. In November 1977 the benefit was payable at a weekly rate of £10.50.

Unemployment Benefit

Unemployment benefit is subject to the 'overlapping benefits' rule in the same way as are sickness and disablement benefits. The benefit is tax free and attracts the earnings-related supplement for six months. Unemployment benefit was payable at £14.70 a week in November 1977: it can be paid for a period up to twelve months. Details of the contribution conditions are given in leaflet NI 12 which you can obtain from your local unemployment benefit office.

You should claim on your first day of unemployment, taking your P 45 (given to you by your employer when you leave) to your local enemployment benefit office. If you do not have your P 45 *DO NOT DELAY* or you may lose benefit. You will be required to register for work as a condition of receiving benefit. If the DHSS feels that you have left your job voluntarily you may be denied benefit (see Section IV on Appeals) but most claims are straightforward.

Maternity Allowance

Maternity allowance is subject to the 'overlapping benefits' rule in the same way as are sickness and disablement benefits. It is tax free and attracts an earning-related supplement. Forms obtainable from your local social security office give detailed instructions on how and when to claim. In November 1977 the standard weekly rate was £14.70.

Maternity Grant

A maternity grant is payable on the birth of a child and entitlement can be based upon either a husband's or a widow's own national insurance contributions. A widow who is pregnant when her husband dies can receive this grant whether or not she is in receipt of a widow's benefit – it is not subject to the overlapping benefits rule. The grant does not affect entitlement to any other benefits.

Child Benefit

Child benefit is a small weekly benefit payable in respect of all children in a family. To be eligible the child must be either under the age of sixteen or under the age of nineteen and still at school, college or university. This benefit involves no contribution conditions nor any means test and is tax free. The amounts and the special arrangements for one-parent families are currently under review. Therefore you should ask for the latest details at your social security or post office. Most widowed mothers will already be receiving child benefit when they are bereaved and therefore no new claim will have to be made.

You will probably find that you have to apply only if you were pregnant when your husband died. To make a claim you complete the form obtainable from a local post office and send it to your local DHSS office. You will receive a book of orders which can be cashed at your local post office.

If you think that you are wrongly denied child benefit you can **appeal** to the local national insurance tribunal. Problems can arise about even a simple benefit like child benefit. For example, the circumstances in which benefit can continue to be paid until a child is nineteen are not always clearcut. If your child decides to leave school at sixteen, and thus you surrender child benefit, but then your child subsequently returns to school because no employment was available you may have difficulty in getting child benefit paid for the period in between. Had your child indicated that he wanted to stay on at school there would have been no query about payment of child benefit during the holidays. (See Section 4 on Appeals.)

Supplementary Benefits

Supplementary benefits are payable by the Supplementary Benefits Commission (part of the DHSS) as of right to people in Great Britain whose incomes are below the level of requirements approved by Parliament each year. You may be entitled to supplementary benefits:
- if you receive no widow's benefits; *or*
- if you do receive widow's benefits

and provided you are not in full-time employment.

Whether you are entitled depends mainly upon your weekly income, your housing costs and the number of dependants you are responsible for. Supplementary benefits are paid in three different ways:
1 **weekly amounts according to your circumstances**
2 **weekly additions according to 'exceptional' circumstances**
3 **lump sum grants to help out with exceptional needs.**

1 **Weekly scale rates** are laid down by Parliament and reviewed each November. The scale rates are the levels below which no household's income should ever fall – and if resources are less than these scale rates the amount of supplementary benefit payable will take that household up to the scale rate level. You can easily work out the correct scale rate for your household by looking at the table on page 31.

2 Whereas the weekly scale rates are laid down by the government each November, **exceptional circumstances additions** are awarded at the discretion of DHSS staff. The staff are given guidelines as to what constitute exceptional circumstances and as to appropriate amounts to give.

Additions are most frequently made for domestic help, a special diet recommended by a doctor, extra heating and high expenditure on laundry. The amount of the special expense is normally calculated on the basis of the actual cost. Where the actual cost is not easy to work out staff take 'standard reckonable expenses' as their guide. For example, the standard reckonable expense of a special diet for a diabetic is £1.75 a week and for renal failure it is £5 a week. Additions for extra heating are standardized at weekly levels according to whether there is, for example chronic illness in the household, difficulty in heating the house due to damp or unusually large rooms. There are also special rates where central heating is used.

Other examples of special expenses are where there is abnormally hard wear and tear of clothing resulting from disability, where furniture storage charges are incurred for good reason, where there are hire purchase commitments for household equipment or furniture which are absolutely essential and for fares to visit a relative in hospital.

When the long-term scale rate is in payment after two years on benefit it includes an element of 50p for extra expenses, and so discretionary additions may be reduced by 50p accordingly.

3   Staff also have discretionary powers to make lump sum grants (or sometimes loans) to meet an exceptional need where the giving of a grant seems to be reasonable. **Exceptional needs payments** (ENPs) cannot be given to people in full-time work but they may be given to people who are not in receipt of weekly benefit – such as widows depending upon their pension. Exceptional needs payments are intended to ensure that no one is left with less than their weekly level of requirements.

When deciding whether to award an ENP, staff ignore any capital you may have up to £200 or if you would be left with less than £200 after paying for the item(s) needed.

Payments are most commonly made for items of clothing – especially shoes. Even though an amount is included in the weekly scale rates towards the replacement of clothing and footwear there are many reasons why and circumstances in which exceptional needs payments will be made. For example, there may be very heavy wear and tear on stockings and shoes as a result of disability: items may have been accidentally burned when using an iron, a child may have lost one shoe! Children outgrow footwear very quickly for example and in recent years inflation has been so great that families living on supplementary benefit simply have not been able to replace shoes out of the weekly allowance.

When payments are made for clothing the amount(s) will be determined by what is known as the standard 'national price list': this is a list issued to officers to guide them as to how much to give. For example, the 1976 list suggested that £4.80 should be given for shoes, £3.25 for a nightdress, £3.95 for a skirt, £6.00 for a dressing gown. Obviously these figures become very quickly out of date as a result of inflation and amounts given have tended to be below what is needed to buy the required items. You will see in the section on Appeals that by going to the supplementary benefit appeal tribunal, amounts can be obtained which are realistic: often officers will themselves allow more than is suggested in the national price list – thus avoiding the need for an appeal.

ENPs can be made in a great variety of situations and it is impossible to describe them all here. The Supplementary Benefits Handbook makes special mention of ENPs for the replacement of bedding, furniture and household equipment, redecoration and repairs, fireguards where there are young children or elderly or infirm people, fares for interviews in connection with looking for work, fares to have a child cared for by relatives or friends, visits to patients in hospital, fuel debts and rent arrears, hire purchase debts, funeral expenses, telephone installation cost for a person living alone and housebound and items needed during emergencies.

You will find a very unusual use made of the ENP scheme mentioned in the Appeals section – a widow had her tax debt cleared!

Claims for supplementary benefit can be made very easily by using the application form on the leaflet SB 1 which you can get from a post office or the local social security office. The National Welfare Benefits Handbook (published by the Child Poverty Action Group (CPAG), 1 Macklin Street, Drury Lane, London WC2; price about 50p) is very helpful, because although in principle entitlement to supplementary benefits might seem to be straight-forward there is a range of circumstances, which we cannot go into here, which means that many more people are entitled than apply. If you are in any doubt about whether you may be entitled it is probably worth applying; there is nothing to lose and you may very well gain. If you are refused benefit when you think you are entitled then it may be worth **appealing** to the Supplementary Benefit Appeal Tribunal. For details of how to do this see the section on Appeals.

If you qualify for weekly scale rate benefits (and exceptional circumstances additions) you will normally receive a book of weekly orders which you can cash at a post office of your choice. There are a number of instances in which the DHSS will decide to make your payments by a giro order which can be cashed at any post office: examples of such instances are payments made soon after you have applied while your order book is being made up; payments made when you are likely to need benefit only for a few weeks – such as while waiting for your widow's benefit order book to come through; payments being made at a time when your financial circumstances are likely to change frequently. Exceptional needs payments are usually made by a giro order which you can cash at your local post office: in the case of furniture the DHSS may obtain second-hand goods for you.

Main Supplementary Benefit Rates (from November 1977)

	Ordinary weekly rate £	Long-term weekly rate * £
Ordinary scale		
Single householder	14.50	17.90
Any other person aged: not less than 18	11.60	14.35
16 to 17	8.90	–
13 to 15	7.40	–
11 to 12	6.10	–
5 to 10	4.95	–
under 5	4.10	–
For blind people		
For any blind person aged: not less than 18	15.75	19.15
16 to 17	9.80	–

* payable after 2 years on benefit. If you or a dependant in your household is aged 80 or over a further 25p is added to these long term rates.

From the above table, list the appropriate amounts for each member of your household and add them up; then add on the cost of your rent and rates (or mortgage interest and rates if you are an owner occupier). The resulting sum is the basic scale rate for your household. If you have any special expenses such as extra heating costs due to young or ill children or because your house is difficult to heat (see next section on Exceptional circumstances additions) then add on the amount by which you think that these extra costs exceed what is 'normal'. You will then have arrived at a figure which represents your total household requirements.

If your weekly income from all sources, but excluding £6 from any part-time earnings, any attendance allowance or education maintenance allowance, is less than the figure representing your total household requirements then you will probably be entitled to supplementary benefit.

(There are special rules governing how any capital you have may be treated and there are other costs which may be taken into account such as hire purchase, house insurance and an element for house repairs; this pamplet cannot deal with all of these items but the Widows' Advisory Service can help you.)

The calculation on the next page shows you how to work out whether you should be receiving supplementary benefit.

Family Income Supplement

Family income supplement (FIS) is a benefit available only to families with a child (or children) where the chief 'breadwinner' is in full-time employment and where the total family income from all sources (excluding childrens' own income, attendance allowance, mobility allowance, rent and rate rebates) is not adequate. Thus if you are a widowed mother but do not receive widowed mother's allowance you will probably have either claimed supplementary benefit or chosen to work. If you have chosen to work full-time you may have wages or a salary below what is called the 'prescribed' amount and therefore be entitled to a weekly supplement – FIS.

To work out whether you are entitled you should follow the procedure set out in the hypothetical case below:

For a Widow With Two Children *

Prescribed amount
(for one adult plus two children) £45.00

Resources
child benefit and earnings £35.00

The amount of FIS payable
is half the difference between the
prescribed amount and resources

$$\frac{£45-35 = £10}{2} \qquad =£5.00$$

*The prescribed amount used in this illustration was the rate in 1977. It varies according to how many children there are.

How to Claim FIS

You can obtain a descriptive leaflet FIS 1 from your local DHSS office or from your post office. You will see that the form is simple to complete and you should send it to the DHSS, Family Income Supplements, Poulton-le-Fylde, Blackpool FY6 8NW. (You should be given a pre-stamped addressed envelope with the leaflet FIS 1.)

You have to send in pay slips or a statement of your accounts, if you are self employed. It is important that you do not delay in making your application if you do not have pay slips or your account to hand; you can send these items on later. If you are eligible for FIS you will receive it from the date of your application, (not from the date when pay slips etc are received by the DHSS) for twelve months in the form of a book of orders which can be

Example of Calculation of Entitlement to Supplementary Benefit

A. Requirements	Weekly amount £
Mrs Widow	14.50
Daughter aged 16 (blind)	9.80
Son aged 14	7.40
Mortgage interest plus rates plus house insurance and repairs allowance	18.67
HP for cooker	1.00
Extra heating allowance	1.40
Special diet allowance for diabetic son	1.75
Total	£54.52

B. Resources	
Widowed mother's allowance - personal rate	17.50
first child	7.40
second child	6.90
Child Benefit	
first child	1.00
second child	1.50
Part-time earnings of £10, less £6 disregarded	4.00
Total	£38.30

C. Entitlement

Entitlement is A – B
Thus £54.52 – 38.30 = £16.22
Mrs Widow would thus receive £16.22 supplementary allowance each week.

cashed each week at your local post office.

You can **renew** your claim for FIS by completing the claim form in your FIS book. This should be done a few weeks before all the orders are used up to make sure that your new book of orders is through by the time you cash the last one in your existing book.

If you are refused FIS and you think that you are eligible or if you think the amount awarded is wrong then you can **appeal** to a local tribunal. The local tribunal is the same one that hears supplementary benefit appeals. You should appeal within 21 days by writing to your local DHSS office saying that you wish to appeal against the FIS decision which you have received. (See section on Appeals.)

The 'Passport' to Other Benefits

If you are entitled to supplementary benefit or FIS you will automatically become entitled also to free prescriptions, free dental treatment, dentures and certain glasses, fares for attending hospital, free legal aid and advice, free school meals for your children and free milk or vitamins if you are pregnant or have children under school age.

Free School Meals

If you are receiving supplementary benefit or family income supplement you should automatically get free school meals for your children.

If you have a low income you may get free school meals for one or more of your children depending upon your circumstances. What the Government defines as a low income is not really low at all! It is certainly well above the levels of widows' benefits. For example, from September 1977 a widow with a *net* income below £0000 was able to receive free school meals for three children. Since school meals cost £1.25 a week per child the value of this benefit can be considerable. The scheme is different from many others mentioned in this Handbook because it is based upon *net* income. To discover what your net income is you deduct from your income items such as tax, national insurance and superannuation payments, rent, rates and mortgage payments, expenses connected with working, life insurance premiums, domestic help and day care costs for pre-school children, the first £6 of your earnings, any attendance allowance, mobility allowance, maternity or death grant and various other outgoings.

You apply for free school meals by obtaining an application form from your local education office or the headteacher at your child's/children's school. Make sure that your completed application form has all your expenses/ deductions etc entered on it.

Education Maintenance Allowances

Education maintenance allowances (EMAs) are not widely publicized and therefore few people get to know of them. They are for schoolchildren, rather like the grants for going to university but they are paid at much lower levels.

Most local education authorities run education maintenance allowance schemes for children who stay on at school or go on to a sixth form college or technical college, where there is no sixth form in the schools. Your child (or children) need not be doing 'O' or 'A' levels to be considered for such an award. The schemes are entirely discretionary and thus there is wide variation in amounts given: some local authortities give nothing, some about £30 and some up to about £200 per year. The grants do not affect entitlement to pensions or supplementary benefit. They are intended to make a contribution to the pupil's maintenance, the cost of uniforms and clothing, the buying of books etc. Pupils can continue to receive free school meals in addition to an EMA.

School Uniform Grants

Most local education authorites run school uniform grant schemes for secondary school children. Each local authority works out its own scheme and the amounts therefore vary widely. Some give as little as £6 every two years: others may give about £50 every year. Some local authorities give uniform grants to those families who are eligible for free school meals: others use a much stiffer means test.

There can be some difficulty if you are receiving supplementary benefit. Sometimes the local authority will try to get the Supplementary Benefits Commission to pay and the SBC will try to get the local authority to pay. If there is a problem it can be resolved by appealing to the Supplementary Benefit Appeal Tribunal. (See section 4 on Appeals.)

Fares to School

Local education authorities have to provide free transport for any child under eight who lives more than 2 miles from his school and for older children who live more than 3 miles from their school.

Local education authorities also have powers to meet the cost of any pupil's 'reasonable travelling expenses'. Therefore, if you have a child/children living within the 2 or 3 mile limits mentioned above for whom the journey perhaps is hazardous on foot or too much of a strain you should approach the authority for help with the cost of fares. If you are in receipt of supplementary benefit and the local education authority refuses help you could apply to the Supplementary Benefits Commission. If the SBC refuses to help then appeal to the local Supplementary Benefit Appeal Tribunal. (See Section 4 on Appeals.)

Boarding Education

If you consider that boarding education would suit the needs of your child/children then you should approach your local education authority for advice. Your local education authority has the powers to meet the full cost of boarding education in special cases and often widowhood is regarded as reason enough for giving this sort of help. Alternatively it may be that your child's (childrens') age, aptitude and ability are such that local day schools cannot provide facilities appropriate to his/her needs. If you want to consider boarding education as a possibility for your child/children then it is up to you to enquire at your local education office.

Free Prescriptions

You may be eligible for free prescriptions depending upon your age, health or income.

If you are sixty or over you get free prescriptions by filling in the declaration on the back of each prescription form.

You can get a certificate which exempts you from charges if
- you are an expectant mother
- you have a child under one
- you suffer from certain medical conditions (listed on form FP 91 which you can get from your local post office or DHSS office)
- you receive supplementary benefit or family income supplement
- your income is not much above supplementary benefit level (you apply by completing form M 11 which you can obtain from your local post office or local DHSS office)

If you are waiting for your Certificate of Exemption and need to get prescriptions then you should pay for them in the normal way but ask for a receipt from the chemist. You can then claim a refund from the DHSS.

If you are an expectant mother you will find an application form for an Exemption Certificate attached to your Certificate of Expected Confinement (form FW8 issued by your doctor, midwife or health visitor); if you have a child aged under one or have a specified medical condition you should complete form FP91 which you obtain from your post office or DHSS office. Children under sixteen get prescriptions free of charge.

Prescription 'season tickets'

If you are not able to get free prescriptions you can buy a season ticket or 'prepayment certificate'. A certificate costing £2 lasts for 6 months and one costing £3.50 lasts for 12 months. If you use prescriptions frequently or have a number of items on each prescription you will find the season ticket gives you quite a saving. You can obtain a season ticket by completing form FP95 which is available in local post offices and local offices of the DHSS.

Free or reduced charges for dental treatment, dentures and glasses

The following groups can receive dental treatment, dentures and glasses free of charge:
- children under sixteen and older children who are still at school;
- expectant mothers and mothers with a child under one (eligible for free dental treatment and dentures only);
- people in receipt of supplementary benefit or family income supplement and those who already hold a valid Certificate of Exemption from prescription charges or who receive free welfare milk/vitamins on grounds of low income.

You do not need to fill in any special form if you are in any of the groups above; you simply have to sign a declaration provided by the dentist or optician.

You may also be entitled to free dental treatment, dentures and glasses or to reduced charges on grounds of low income. If your income is not more than about £2.50 above supplementary benefit level you should be entitled to these services free of charge. If you think that you may be eligible then you should ask your dentist for form F1D or your optician for form F1; you fill in the form and send it to your local DHSS office in the envelope which should be provided for you.

Free welfare milk and vitamins

If you are an expectant mother or have more than two children under school age you will be entitled to free welfare milk and vitamins. If you have a physically or mentally handicapped child between the ages five and sixteen who is not attending school you should get form FW20 from your local DHSS office in order to claim welfare milk.

If you get supplementary benefit or family income supplement you should automatically be receiving free welfare milk and vitamins for yourself if you are pregnant and for any children under school age. If you have not received them then complete the blue form A9 which is in your weekly order book and send it to your local DHSS office.

If your income is not more than about £2.50 above supplementary benefit level and you are either pregnant or have children under school age then you should apply on form M11 which you can obtain from your local post office or local DHSS office.

Fares to hospital

If you go to hospital as an in-patient or as an out-patient you may be able to get help with the cost of fares for each visit. If you get supplementary benefit or family income supplement your application will automatically be approved. If your *net* income is not much above supplementary benefit level then you will probably also get help. (Net income is arrived at by deducting the sort of outgoings mentioned in the section on free school meals – ie items such as tax,

insurance, rent, mortgage rates, etc) if you are an in-patient you should fill in
form H1 at least seven days before discharge – the hospital will provide you
with the form and will send it to the DHSS for you. If you are awaiting
admission as an in-patient or going to be an out-patient then you should ask
the hospital for form 2566 before your appointment/admission and take it or
send it to your local office of the DHSS. If you are eligible the DHSS will
make arrangements for the hospital to refund you your fares. If you need
the money before you go you should make this clear when you apply. If the
hospital states that you need an escort then his/her fares can be applied for
too.

Fares to visit relatives in hospital

If you get supplementary benefit or family income supplement or if your
income is not much above supplementary benefit level then the DHSS
may be able to help you meet the cost of fares to visit a close relative in
hospital – a child or a parent, brother or sister, for example. Even if the hospital
is some distance away – perhaps involving an overnight stay – expenses can, in
exceptional circumstances, be met.

You should make an application direct to your local DHSS office.

INCOME TAX

Many widows experience problems with the Inland Revenue. Most widows
have never had to deal with income tax matters before their husband died:
most widows have to deal with income matters after the death of their
husband. Some problems associated with income tax can be avoided if you
know what to do and when to do it.

Income tax matters are rarely as complicated as they are rumoured to be.
Always check with your local tax office if you are not sure about anything. If
you feel fairly energetic you can read about income tax in any one of a range
of good, widely available publications designed for the lay person. (See list of
Useful Publications in Section 5).

The main reason for widows experiencing difficulties with the income tax
authorities is that widow's benefits are taxable. In recent years even a widow
who does not work may find that her level of widow's benefit is such that she
has to pay a small amount of tax on it. Any widow who does work will find
that she is taxed on the whole of her earnings – unlike her married co-worker
who pays tax on only a part of her pay. If the Inland Revenue are informed of
your husband's death promptly then you will find that adjustments are made
so that you do not experience problems; if you delay in informing the Inland
Revenue about your husband's death then you may find that you quickly get
into 'tax arrears' and thus receive a hefty demand from the tax collector.

When you inform the tax office that your husband has died (and your own
tax office if you are working) the Inspector will ask you to estimate the
amount of any benefits (widow's allowance, earnings related widow's
supplementary allowance etc) you are likely to receive. You can find out how
much these are likely to be by asking at your local Social Security office.
When the Inspector has this information, but not before, he will try to
estimate how much tax will be due up to the end of the financial year (5 April
after the death of your husband). If you are working he will adjust your tax
code (which reflects the value of your allowances and tax reliefs) so that by
the end of the financial year you should have paid the correct amount of tax.

If you are not working the Inspector will be able to tell you whether you are likely to be liable for any tax, if so approximately how much and how this should be paid.

If you see the income tax authorities as soon as possible after your husband's death you will almost certainly avoid any major problems.

The tax due on the period up to the date of your husband's death will have been deducted from his wages or salary if he was employed; if he was self-employed there may be tax due, and normally this will be settled by the executors or administrators on the winding up of the estate. If you have any doubts – whether your husband was employed or self-employed – then contact your local Inspector of Taxes.

The golden rule is always to inform the authorities of changes in your circumstances and always to check that you know what demands will be made of you, if any.

The Inland Revenue publish a very useful short guide called *Income Tax and Widows* (Leaflet number I.R.23). This leaflet is not revised very often and therefore you should take any figures mentioned in it only as a guide; every time the budget changes our tax allowances and the rates of taxation this leaflet becomes out of date. (For example, at the time of writing the leaflet currently available was dated 1976).

You will see from the leaflet that the following items of income are liable to be taxed:

widow's national insurance benefits
widow's allowance, widowed mother's allowance, widow's pension, war widow's pension (though only 50 per cent of this is taxable), industrial death benefit etc.

all other pensions and annuities
– retirement pensions, pensions from your husband's employment etc.

wages, salaries and income from self-employment interest, dividends etc.

Some items of income are *not* taken into account when working out your tax liability:
– national insurance sickness and unemployment benefits
– invalidity benefit and attendance allowance
– child's allowance and rent allowance payable with a war widow's pension
– also child benefit (but this was not mentioned in the 1976 leaflet).

The way your tax liability is calculated is the same as for anyone else:
1 your annual income from all sources will be added up – say £1,500
2 you will be given 'personal allowances' and tax relief on certain items of expenditure (such as interest on your mortgage, certain insurance policies) adding up to – say £1,250
3 your tax due would then be calculated by taking 2 from 1, in this case £250, and charging tax at the relevant rate – say 30 per cent which would, in this hypothetical example give a tax liability of £75 for the year on the original income of £1,500. (At the time of writing the tax rate was 34 per cent.)

If you are over pensionable age you will be given a single person's tax allowance; when you reach the age of sixty five you will be given a higher personal allowance called an 'age allowance'. When you are between the age of sixty and sixty-five you may find that you have the choice as to whether to continue to receive your widow's pension or whether to change to a retirement pension; your choice will probably depend largely on whether you intend to work. Until recently a widow who was working or intended to work full-time after the age of sixty would have found that she was better off drawing a widow's pension because, although the pension is taxed it is not reduced according to earnings. However, the government is gradually phasing out the 'earnings rule' on retirement pensions – so that the retirement pension will no longer be reduced according to earnings or withdrawn completely when women work full-time or have high income from work. Thus there will soon be no difference between the treatment of widow's and retirement pensions. If you think that you may be affected in this way you should enquire at your local DHSS office; this is not a choice affected by tax.

If you are under pensionable age you will be given a single person's tax allowance. If you have a child or children you will also be given an 'additional personal allowance' which will bring the total allowances up to the same level as those of a married man. You will, of course, in addition be able to claim the income tax child allowances for any child or children. The income tax child allowances vary according to the age of the child and according to whether the child is the first, second or subsequent child in your family. These income tax child allowances are currently being phased out and replaced by the non-taxable Child Benefit (see section on Child Benefit). Income tax child allowances are affected by the child's own income but the new Child Benefit will not be so affected.

It is important to check that the Inland Revenue have given you all your allowances and that they have all the information necessary to give you these. Therefore it is important to arrange for the tax office to send you the leaflet which gives the amounts of all the allowances – eg leaflet BP(1977) describes the rates of personal allowances introduced by the chancellor in his March budget.

Methods of collection of tax

You will find that tax is not deducted from your widow's benefit, before you receive it. Any tax due will be collected in one of two ways. If you are not working you will be asked to pay a specified amount four times a year. If you are working you will find that tax will be deducted from your wages or salary at a rate that takes into account your widow's benefit. Thus a working widow receives less in her pay packet than a single or married woman doing the same job for the same pay. The reason for this is that the single or married woman will not be in receipt of a taxable pension in addition to her pay. Many widows feel that this is very unfair and that the pension should be tax free. No government has yet felt able to make pensions tax free but some tax concessions are given to war widows.

When a lump sum payment is requested by the Collector of Taxes – this will be from the non-working widow and sometimes from the working widow who for some reason gets into arrears – you can ask for extra time to pay if the amounts being requested will cause you financial hardship. By asking for extra time you can pay smaller amounts on the four occasions during the year when your tax becomes due. You will see in the Appeals Section (page 50) mention of a case of hardship where the widow had so little income from her pension and supplementary benefit that the DHSS actually agreed to pay her tax bill! This strange situation arose because the 'tax threshold' has fallen so low in recent years that widows without extra tax reliefs and without children have almost certainly fallen into the tax paying bracket even if they have not been at work.

Sometimes a widow who is working and who has tax arrears may repay the tax due by having more deducted from her wages or salary each week or month than would otherwise be due. Again, if the amount being deducted leaves you with too little on which to live it is worth asking the Inspector of Taxes to make an adjustment so that you can pay it off more slowly.

Mistakes by the Inland Revenue

Sometimes staff of the Inland Revenue do like the rest of us, make mistakes. Since 1971 the Inland Revenue have adopted the practice of ignoring tax arrears which arise through official error. Thus if it is established that in your case there has been an official error you should make representation to the Inland Revenue asking that such tax arrears are not collected. At the time of writing the Inland Revenue are not collecting any arrears arising from official error where the gross income is less than £3,000 per year; where the gross income is between £3,000 and £6,000 half of the arrears are collected. If the gross income is more than £6,000 or if there is investment income of £500 or more (and a gross income of £3,000 or more) attempts are made by the Inland Revenue to collect the whole of the arrears.

In practice the Inland Revenue will not try to recover arrears arising out of official error if hardship would thus be caused. By official error it is meant that the Inland Revenue have received the information which is necessary to enable a correct assessment of tax liability to be made but that such information has not been used appropriately or within a reasonable period of time.

For example, a widow who approached the Widows Advisory Service received a tax demand for £227.94. It was eventually discovered that the Inland Revenue had failed to take account of her widow's pension when revising her tax code. The Advisory Service made representations on her behalf and the Inland Revenue withdrew the tax demand.

HOUSING

Owned homes

Where your husband has left your family home to you in his will you should be in a very secure position provided that;
– his estate is solvent, *and*
– *either* there is a mortgage protection policy *or* you can afford to keep up the mortgage repayments.

If your husband left debts and no other property from which the debts can be paid it may be necessary to sell the house in order to pay them. Many mortgages are protected by an insurance policy which means that the mortgage debt is either automatically paid off on your husband's death or that there is a sum of insurance money set aside for this purpose; thus the ownership of your home should be automatically transferred to you. If there is no such insurance policy then you may find that, in order to stay in the home, you will have to find enough money to continue the mortgage repayments. If you have difficulty in finding enough money to do this you should check whether you may be entitled to supplementary benefit (see section on supplementary benefits) or whether the building society will extend the period of the mortgage so that the repayments become lower and within your resources.

If your husband left no will or if his will is invalid (known as dying intestate) then you will be entitled to succeed to some or all of his property and you will be able to ask that the home be transferred to your name.

If your husband did leave a valid will in which the home was left to someone else then you will have to ask the court to make 'reasonable provision' for you from your husband's estate (see the section on wills, probate and intestacy).

Rented homes

You may be living in *either* a protected *or* an unprotected home. Most privately rented furnished and unfurnished homes are protected; council homes are not protected. If you are a protected tenant then you have the right to take over the tenancy provided that you were living with your husband at the time of his death (ie you were not separated). You may already have a joint tenancy in which case the tenancy will automatically be transferred to you. If you live in a council house then it is up to your local council as to whether the tenancy is either already in your joint names or can be transferred into your name. Most councils will transfer your home into your name; sometimes you may be asked to move to smaller alternative accommodation if this is appropriate to your circumstances.

If there are any problems you should go to a solicitor, the local Citizens' Advice Bureau or to a Housing Action Group if there is one in your area, or to the Widows Advisory Service (WAS).

Rate rebates, rent allowances and rent rebates

Owner occupiers, council and private tenants may be eligible for a rate rebate; this applies whether or not you pay rates directly. (For example many council tenants do not realize that they pay rates because a weekly amount is included with the rent; but they are treated in exactly the same way as owner occupiers for rebate purposes.)

Rent rebates are available to council and new town tenants: rent allowances are available to private tenants.

Eligibility for rent rebates, rent allowances and rate rebates depends upon:
- your rates and/or rent
- your income, and
- the number of dependants that you have.

The Department of the Environment publishes a leaflet called *How to Pay Less Rates* which you can obtain from your local council or Citizens' Advice Bureau; this explains in detail how to work out whether you are entitled. For example, in November 1976 a single person with a weekly income of £15 and weekly rates of £1 received a rebate of £1; a single parent with three children, and income of £60 per week and rates of £3.50 a week received a rebate of £1.43 per week.

In November 1976, a widow on her own with a rent of £4.00 per week and an income of less than £35.95 received a rent rebate; a widow parent with three children and a rent of £9.00 per week received a rebate if her income was less than £79.35 per week. The amount of the rebate is determined by how far the actual income fell below the weekly incomes mentioned above – the lower the income the greater the rebate. The income levels which guide entitlement to rate and rent rebates and allowances are raised regularly and if you think that you may be eligible you should go along to your local rates or housing department or write asking for an application form. It is almost always worth applying; you may have a lot to gain *and you certainly will lose nothing by applying.*

Rate rebates are usually made by reducing your rates – or if you have already paid them you will receive a cash refund.

Rent rebates are usually made by reducing the rent.

Rent allowances are usually made by giving a cash payment (ie your landlord need never know that you are getting a rent allowance).

Applications should be made as soon as possible. You can only receive a rebate or allowance backdated to the relevant week or period in which you applied. If you are working you will need to send in pay slips but if you do not have them to hand do not delay your application: send them on later.

You should receive a written notice showing how your entitlement (or non-entitlement) has been decided. If you think that your local council has made a mistake or been unfair you should write within a month giving your reasons. The council should then write to you again giving you its final decision. If you are still not satisfied then you can take up the matter with a local councillor or write, giving details, to the Widows Advisory Service.

Note: rebates, allowances and supplementary benefit

If you are in receipt of supplementary benefit then the amount you receive each week will take account of your rebates/allowances if these are in payment or will cover the whole of the rates and/or rent if you have no rebates/allowances.

EDUCATION, TRAINING AND RE-TRAINING

Many widows find that they not only need to earn money to supplement their pension but that they need a regular point of contact outside the home. Some will have worked during their married life, others gave up work on marriage and never returned. Work is not necessarily the answer to all the problems of widowhood but many can find work stimulating and satisfying. Whether you have worked before or not you may feel that you would like to explore new openings.

The Department of Employment offers a free and confidential **vocational guidance** service for anyone who is over eighteen and needs help in finding out what kind of work would suit them. Major cities have Employment Services Agencies and you can make an appointment by contacting your nearest unit direct or by asking at your local job centre or employment office.

There are a number of other organizations which specialize in vocational guidance but which charge fees ranging from £20 to £40. A complete list is produced by the Advisory Centre for Education called *Organizations Offering Vocational Guidance*, price 25p. To obtain this you should write to ACE, Dr White House, 32 Trumpington Street, Cambridge CB2 1QY.

Returners, price 85p and obtainable from the National Advisory Centre on Careers for Women, 251, Brompton Road, London SW3 (01-589 9237) contains practical advice, information about opportunities for both qualified and unqualified people and useful addresses.

Your choice of work or career may involve obtaining some additional qualifications. Your local technical college or college of **further education** will run courses at basic and advanced levels. For example, you could study for 'O' and 'A' levels either during the day or at evening classes. You can look up what courses are available in the CRAC *Directory of Further Education* which should be in your local library.

You can also look up the CRAC/CBI Yearbook *Education and Training* which lists vocational training courses at colleges of further education and polytechnics. Again, courses can be taken full-time or part-time or in the evenings and lead to qualifications such as those recognized by the Royal Society of Arts and City and Guilds. They will equip you for employment, for example, as a hairdresser, computer programmer or plumber. For many of these courses you do not need to have 'O' or 'A' levels.

The *Personnel and Training Year Book* (look for it in your local library) lists
apprenticeship and training schemes; the *Education Committees Year Book*
gives a list of Industrial Training Boards and their local regional training
officers. From these sources you can find out about training 'on the job'.

You may be surprised to learn that you may be able to take a course of
professional training without 'O' and 'A' levels. There are now many courses
which admit mature students and waive the usual entry requirements. For
example, if you would like to train for social work you may be able to get a
job as an unqualified social worker with your local social services department;
the department may then 'second' you for professional training on a two year
course at a polytechnic or university, and secondment would be on full pay.
Many women who train in this way do not have 'O' and 'A' levels and
although they feel very nervous at the start of the course about their ability to
write essays again (after perhaps thirty years away from education) they
usually fall into the routine very quickly and do very well. It is enthusiasm and
commitment which tend to count rather than past proven academic ability. If
you want to train for a profession you should write direct to the professional
body concerned (look up the address in your local library) and find out what
qualifications, if any, are required and where courses are provided. You will
also be able to find out whether there are grants and/or secondment to cover
the period of training.

You may wish to study for a **degree** at a university or polytechnic. As a
mature student you will find many universities and polytechnics which will
consider applications from women without the usual two 'A' levels. You can
find out about courses by looking at *Choosing a University*, or *Which
University?* in your local library. You can obtain a handbook on admissions
procedure to universities from UCCA, P O Box 28, Cheltenham, Glos. GL50
1HY price 40p. The *Compendium of Degree Courses* in polytechnics is free
and can be obtained from the Council for National Academic Awards,
344-354 Gray's Inn Road, London WC1 8BB.

If you think that you might be interested in taking a degree course and if
you have not studied for some years then it is always worth registering for,
say, one 'A' level at your local college of further education or registering for a
Workers Educational Association (WEA) course – just to demonstrate your
enthusiasm for a return to study and to get the 'feel' of education again.

If you do not like the idea of becoming a student alongside a lot of school
leavers then you might like to consider the Open University. The Open
University runs degree courses by correspondence and by providing radio and
television programmes which support the course material. You do not need
any formal qualifications to become an Open University student. Students are
accepted on the basis of 'first come first served' – therefore the earlier you
apply the more likely you are to be accepted. The Open University offers a
wide range of choices and you can 'mix' arts, social science, science,
technology, mathematics and education studies courses. The degree scheme is
organized on a 'credit basis' which means you choose how many credits you
think that you can do in any one year and thus *you* determine how long it
takes you to get your degree. This flexibility can be very helpful – for
example, if you want to do one course in one year but feel that you can
cope with two and a half in another year. If you already have some
qualifications you may be given 'credit exemptions' and therefore need only
two or three years to get your degree.

In the Open University system you will certainly find co-students of your
own age group (even if you are in your sixties or seventies) and you will have

an opportunity to meet them at your local 'study centre' – usually a few rooms set aside in a college of further education or a polytechnic or university. You will also have some contact with tutors – the staff who mark your essays.

For further information about the Open University you should write to P O Box 48, Milton Keynes MK7 6AB.

The National Extension College provides **correspondence tuition** at a wide range of levels, from GCE ordinary and advanced levels, to University of London external degrees and some professional qualifications. There are many correspondence colleges and a complete list is available for 25p from ACE, Dr White House, 32 Trumpington Street, Cambridge CB2 1QY.

There are very many openings for further study and training which cannot be mentioned here. If none of the above suit your needs then contact the Widows Advisory Service at the Voluntary Service Centre, Chell Road, Stafford, ST1 2QA.

Financing your education, training or re-training

Money can seem to be a problem if you want to continue your education or train/re-train. However, there are many sources of finance to-day and you should *never* be deterred from applying for a course because you do not have the money.

Local education authorities are obliged to give a grant to anyone who has two 'A' levels and is offered a place in a university, college of education or polytechnic for a degree course or certain recognised courses. The amount of the grant, including increases for dependants, should be quite adequate for your needs although you might be distressed to discover that the amount you receive will take into account any widow's benefit.

Your local education authority can also give 'discretionary' awards: these are awards for a range of courses, including degree courses taken by mature students who do not have the requisite 'A' levels, taken at colleges of education, technical colleges, polytechnics and universities. The generosity of local education authorities does vary but it is always worth making an enquiry. Local authorities may also help with the costs of doing an Open University course.

There are many other sources of finance for educational courses. The National Union of Students, 3 Endsleigh Street, London WCLH ODU produces two useful leaflets: *Mature Women's Grants,* price 10p and *Educational Charities,* price 15p. ACE produces a comprehensive guide *Grants for Higher Education* and you should find this in your local library.

The National Advisory Centre on Careers for Women at 251 Brompton Road, London SW3 (01-589 9237) and the Society for Promoting the Training of Women at Court Farm, Hedgerley, Slough, Bucks SL2 3UY both give interest-free loans to women and repayment does not start until you are working.

The government Training Opportunities Scheme (TOPS) provides courses for people who are not eligible for a grant towards training or retraining. There arc more than 500 courses provided in Skill centres, colleges of education and by employers. The TOPS scheme is linked to local job centres run by the Employment Services Agency which help with finding work after the course is completed. The TOPS scheme creates opportunities in a very wide field – training is offered in business administration, secretarial and commercial work, craft and technical skills in engineering and construction, and in television/ electronics and many other skills; postgraduate courses in management are available in certain circumstances too.

Whilst doing a TOPS course you receive a tax-free allowance, plus allowances for dependants, travel and other expenses, free midday meals, and your national insurance contribution is paid. However, as a widow you cannot get the full tax free allowance *and* continue to draw your widow's benefit. But you can choose to continue to receive your widow's benefit and a special 'abated' training allowance. The choice depends entirely upon your financial circumstances and the Widows Advisory Service can guide you on this. Many widows have started TOPS courses and then have given up before completion – because they have not made the correct choice: do not let this happen to you.

4 Appeals

NATIONAL INSURANCE, CHILD BENEFIT, SUPPLEMENTARY BENEFIT AND FIS

Sometimes you may think you have been treated wrongly or unfairly when applying for either supplementary benefits, family income supplement, child benefit or national insurance benefit; sometimes you may even find that your benefit has been stopped and you may not understand why or you may consider that the Department of Health and Social Security has wrongly withdrawn your benefit. In these circumstances you have a right of appeal.

You can appeal to a local supplementary benefit or a local national insurance appeal tribunal. Such tribunals are totally independent of the DHSS and appeals are usually heard by three people, a chairman and two members. Appeals are informal and you should be given as much time as you wish to explain your appeal and to be heard sympathetically. The appeals tribunal system is a safeguard against mistakes being made by DHSS officials and often allows information to be presented that DHSS officials have not asked for but which is relevant to your circumstances. Tribunals exist to be used and have been used successfully by many widows.

You can appeal against any decision of an official of the DHSS. In the case of supplementary benefits this can even be a verbal decision; in the case of national insurance this must be a written decision. You can appeal, normally within 21 days of the decision, simply in writing by saying that you wish to appeal against the decision to . . .(eg refuse benefit) taken on . . . (date) and hand this in at your local DHSS office. If your appeal is about national insurance or child benefit you will be given a proper form on which to appeal.

Common examples are as follows: appeals against refusal to award supplementary benefits or widows' benefits, appeals about the amounts awarded, appeals against the withdrawal of benefits, appeals about alleged cohabitation. You will see in the examples that follow how widows' have appealed and won their cases.

A week before an appeal hearing is due you will receive the 'tribunal papers'. These papers set out your reasons for appealing, the reasons why the DHSS took the original decision and the law behind the DHSS decision. Usually these papers come through about three weeks after you lodge an appeal about supplementary benefits and perhaps as much as three months after you lodge a national insurance appeal. Since these papers arrive only about one week before the date on which your hearing is set down to be heard, you will either have to think quickly in order to prepare your case or you have to ask for an adjournment – i e ask that the date for the hearing is postponed (you will find discussion as to when it is appropriate to do this in some of the examples that follow). These papers are very important because often you will not find out the reasons for the original decision until the papers arrive.

Many widows try to get a friend, social worker or member of the Widows

Advisory Service to help them with their case; you cannot get legal aid and therefore it is quite expensive to employ a solicitor to help you. When you receive the tribunal papers you will see that there is a reply slip on which you indicate whether you want to be present at the hearing of your case and which enables you to say whether you intend to be represented. If you do take along a friend or social worker etc. then indicate that you will be represented when you complete this reply slip. You can also use the reply slip to request an adjournment if you want a little more time, perhaps to find someone to help you.

It is always important to attend your hearing or to get someone to go in your place. The members of the tribunal will otherwise make their decision on the basis of the DHSS papers alone – and obviously you are not likely to win in this situation. If you attend you can explain your position, mention any relevant evidence, discuss why you think the DHSS has been wrong; in this situation you can expect a fair hearing.

You will have your expenses associated with attending the hearing reimbursed on the spot. If you work you will also have your loss of earnings reimbursed. If the appeal is to do with supplementary benefits then any friend, relation or volunteer who attends to help you will have his/her expenses/loss of earnings reimbursed too. In national insurance appeals it is not quite so straightforward; if the Tribunal feel that your representatives have helped the tribunal in reaching their decision then they may award expenses and loss of earnings.

Hearings usually take place in a building which is quite independent of the DHSS office. Therefore it is important to read carefully the documents telling you where to go and the date of the hearing. It is also important to try to arrive on time. If you are late the tribunal may proceed without you.

If you find that you are going to be late it is important to try to ring a message through; you probably will not have a telephone number for the building where the tribunal is meeting; therefore ring your local DHSS office and insist that a message be conveyed immediately to the clerk to the tribunal – preferably indicating how late you are likely to be.

When you get to the office where the tribunal are meeting you will find notices indicating the waiting room. Sit in there are wait for the clerk. If there is a hearing in progress the clerk will be in with the tribunal members. He/she will come out when the hearing finishes. The clerk will approach you and ask for your name and will ask who are your representatives. You should then be asked what expenses and loss of earnings you have incurred. If the clerk forgets this it is worth asking. If you forget, then remember when you come out or, if necessary, write afterwards.

You may find that you have to wait for the hearing. Often the proceedings get behind schedule. Clerks may often arrange hearings in quick succession because most appellants do not turn up for their hearings. If several appellants take along a representative, or if all appellants attend then the programme can easily get delayed. Since you will want to have a full and fair hearing do not get upset if this should be the case.

The clerk may have arranged anything between five and ten hearings for any one morning or afternoon session. The members of the tribunal do not hear appeals as part of their full time employment – essentially they are volunteers too (the Chairman gets a fee, the members get expenses only) – and thus are there for only a morning or perhaps a 2 session day. Since many appellants do not turn up for their hearings you will find that many chairmen and members not only welcome the presence of the person appealing but also welcome representatives.

When the tribunal members are ready to receive you the clerk will call you from the waiting room. There will be enough chairs for you and your

representative and for witnesses if you or the DHSS have decided they are
necessary. The tribunal members will be sitting on one side of the table and
you will be asked to sit on the opposite side. There will be the clerk at one end
and usually beside the clerk the 'presenting officer' or 'insurance officer' from
the DHSS.

The chairman should explain that the tribunal is independent and wishes to
give you a fair hearing. Usually the chairman will ask the spokesman from the
DHSS to read out the reasons for the original decision and to mention any
relevant facts and law. The chairman will ask you or your representative to
explain why you are appealing and why you think your appeal should succeed.
The chairman and members may ask both the DHSS representative and you
and your representative (and witnesses) questions.

If you are at a supplementary benefit appeal tribunal you will be asked to
leave when everyone has said all that is necessary; the tribunal clerk will send
you the written decision of the tribunal within a few days of the hearing. If
you are at a national insurance appeal hearing the clerk will ask you to leave
the room and wait for a while. You will then either be called back into the
hearing room for, or the clerk will bring to you, the decision of the tribunal.
This is only in brief form and full details will be sent on to you a few days
later. If the tribunal finds against you you will be given details of how to
appeal to the National Insurance Commissioner. That means, if you have lost
your case before the local national insurance tribunal, you have a right of
appeal to a superior body. (If you lose an appeal to a local supplementary
benefit appeal tribunal you have no further rights, except on a point of law to
the High Court.)

Not many people appeal to the National Insurance Commissioner. No-one
knows why. It may be that people who lose their appeals at local level simply
feel that they may have no case to take further. However, the National
Association of Widows has helped a number of widows to take their case to
the Commissioner and you will see reference to this in one of the examples
cited. If you want to **appeal to the National Insurance Commissioner** then
approach the Widows Advisory Service for help.

If you win your appeal any money due to you (perhaps your benefit has
been stopped for a time or perhaps you should have been receiving more) will
be backdated to the date of your appeal to the local national insurance
tribunal or the date when, for example, benefit was stopped.

EXAMPLES OF CASES TAKEN TO APPEAL

The examples that follow have been selected to show you what sort of issues
have come to appeal, both before national insurance and supplementary
benefit appeal tribunals. Widow's benefit can only be denied on grounds of
alleged cohabitation (or re-marriage, but that is not a problem here!) and
therefore some detailed attention has been given to it. Most people who appeal
have not been denied benefits completely but have queries about the amount
of benefit.

What is Cohabitation?

You will see from the notes at the back of your order book of benefits that as
a widow you cannot continue to be entitled to benefit if you re-marry or if
you 'cohabit with a man as his wife'. The reasoning behind this is that widow's

benefits are intended to compensate for the loss of a husband's earnings and other support; thus if you re-marry or cohabit you should not be treated differently from other married couples. Likewise, if you are claiming supplementary benefit the same rule applies; supplementary benefit (scale rate) is payable according to household resources and if you are living with a man who is in full-time work you have no entitlement to benefit.

You will probably consider that such a rule is fair and just. But there are problems with administering the rule and many widows are accused of cohabiting when in fact they are not. The Widows Advisory Service has received many letters from widows who have taken in lodgers to supplement their income and subsequently their pension or other benefit has suddenly stopped. It is in this sort of situation that an appeal often becomes necessary.

The following examples illustrate the sort of circumstances in which cohabitation may be alleged by the DHSS and where on appeal the widow concerned is found not to be cohabiting.

Mrs A had 4 children, two girls and two boys. She was drawing a widowed mother's allowance. One day, without warning, an official of the DHSS called at her house and demanded that she hand him her order book. When she asked why she should do this he said that the DHSS had reason to believe that she was cohabiting. The circumstances of the case were that about a year after her husband's death a long-standing family friend (male) was desperate for somewhere to live as his marriage had broken up. Mrs A agreed to take him in as a lodger even though he had to share a bedroom with her two sons. (It was a small house and there was no spare bedroom.) He was quite happy with this arrangement; he could not find alternative accommodation in the area and his work was in the area. Occasionally he helped Mrs A with heavy work – some of the decorating and some of the gardening. He and Mrs A went to church together and both sang in the church choir. He ate his meals with the family and Mrs A did his washing for him. He watched the family television.

The DHSS argued that these circumstances constituted cohabitation. Mrs A was distraught. Eventually she got in touch with the Widows Advisory Service and appealed to the local National Insurance Appeal Tribunal. It took a long time for her appeal to be heard; she was without her widowed mother's allowance for more than six months and had to borrow from relations. At her hearing she explained that she did not have a marriage relationship with the lodger; she explained the ways in which her marriage relationship had been very different from the present relationship. The vicar came along as a witness. The two elder children also came along as witnesses. The tribunal decided that she was not cohabiting.

It appeared that the DHSS were made suspicious of Mrs A because they received an anonymous letter from the lodger's ex-wife. Eventually Mrs A received a new widowed mother's allowance order book and money backdated to the day her book had been withdrawn.

The case of **Mrs C** was lost at the hearing before the local National Insurance Tribunal. She had attended with her solicitor. She asked the Widows Advisory Service to represent her before the National Insurance Commissioner. It was clear that her solicitor had not had much experience of dealing with this sort of case but in any event it is quite possible that the facts that were brought to light before the Commissioner would have not been revealed earlier. It is difficult for the widow appealing and for her representative to elicit all relevant facts.

Mrs C worked and was in receipt of a widow's pension. She lived in an area of dire housing shortage and could not find anywhere satisfactory to rent. A man with whom she worked was in the same position regarding accommodation. They decided to jointly buy a house. Her case was further complicated by the fact that for a time she assumed the surname of the man after moving to the house – as she put it, 'to avoid gossip'. Thus, in a sense it is hardly surprising that the local tribunal 'found against' her.

However, when her appeal to the Commissioner was put there were many additional facts available. Mrs C and the man in question had genuinely set up two households. They each had their own part of the house – their own sitting room, their own bedroom. The degree to which this was the case had not been explored by the DHSS officer; neither she nor her solicitor had made much of this before the local tribunal. But the Widows Advisory Service representative saw how crucial this sort of information was to the case. Evidence such as the fact that they had two irons, two fridges, two vacuum cleaners was made available to the Commissioner. The fact that they had independent social lives was also explored. Witnesses were called to vouch for various facts.

It took eighteen months for Mrs C's case to be cleared up. She had her pension book restored and received backdated money from when her book had been withdrawn. During this time she had gone through agony; she lost two stones in weight. But all along she had felt that the DHSS had not understood the situation correctly.

What is good cause for a late claim?

For most national insurance benefits there are time limits within which you must make your claim. For example, to make a valid claim for widow's allowance you must apply within three months of your husband's death.

However, it is possible to make a late claim if you can show 'good cause' for the delay. Sometimes it is not possible to convince the local DHSS office that you did have good cause for submitting your claim late and thus you may have to appeal to the local National Insurance Appeal Tribunal.

One rather unusual case illustrates this. A widow felt that her husband should have received sickness benefit for nine months prior to his death (he died from cancer). She approached the Widow's Advisory Service for help.

The husband had tried to get sickness benefit but had failed because his doctor did not believe that he was unfit for employment and would therefore not issue a sick note. It was not until shortly before he died that the illness was diagnosed. Therefore the widow was advised to put in a late claim, on behalf of her deceased husband, for sickness benefit during the relevant period. She was advised to argue that there was good cause for a late claim; circumstances had subsequently shown that had the illness been diagnosed earlier the husband would undoubtedly have been given the medical evidence required to make a successful application for sickness benefit. Therefore, she argued before the tribunal that her husband had not been able to get 'sick notes' because at the time the doctor refused to give them. The tribunal found the argument convincing and paid to her the sickness benefit that her husband would have received had the doctor known his condition.

What is 'sickness'?

Sickness benefit can be denied to people who the DHSS feels are not sick and to people who it is felt are engaging in activities which are 'prejudicial to recovery'. An example of the former is given below and an example of the latter might be gardening when off sick due to a back injury!

A widow approached the Advisory Service when she had been denied sickness benefit; her sick note from her doctor cited 'bereavement' as her illness. Thus she did not receive either the sickness benefit or the earnings related supplement to which she would otherwise have been entitled nor would her employer pay her sick benefit!

However, advice was given to approach the DHSS again and since the doctor was actually treating her with tranquillizers she did eventually receive her sickness benefit and earnings related supplement, backdated to the relevant periods after the beginning of her incapacity to work. In this case an appeal to the local national insurance tribunal was not necessary: the DHSS 'reviewed their original decision' without seeking confirmation of a tribunal. Had this widow not protested she would have lost over £50 in benefit due to her.

If your doctor marks a sick note 'bereavement' do mention that this term may cause difficulties.

(Note that this widow was entitled to sickness benefit because her widow's benefit was not payable at the full rate due to insufficient contributions having been made by her husband.)

What is Voluntary Unemployment?

A recently bereaved widow who was working decided to move in order to be nearer her family. On settling into her new home and town she experienced difficulty in finding employment immediately and therefore applied for unemployment benefit (she was only in receipt of an age-related pension).

However, the DHSS denied her unemployment benefit on the grounds that she had left her previous job 'voluntarily and without just cause'.

In due course the widow's appeal was heard by a local tribunal and the tribunal felt that this widow had a very good reason for giving up her previous job and moving to be near to her family. Thus she received unemployment benefit and earnings related supplement in respect of the short period (only two weeks) while she was without a job.

What is the Overlapping Benefits rule?

A widow decided to take a TOPS course. She had been in receipt of widowed mother's allowance since she had two school age children. She had the choice of continuing to receive her widowed mother's allowance plus a small 'abated' training allowance or claiming the full training allowance (tax free) plus allowances for her children. On the advice given she decided to opt for the training allowance because she thought that she would be better off. However, to her dismay, she found that the amount of her training allowance was reduced when she took time off from her course to look after the children at half term, to take children to the dentist etc. In some weeks her income was so low that she just could not manage. Her case was taken to the local national insurance appeal tribunal and it was argued that in any week she should have received 'the higher' of the two benefits to which she was entitled; the tribunal authorized backpayment of a sum (over £50) to cover the weeks when she had been short.

What is a householder?

A widow shared her house with her 55 year-old son who worked. She was too old to be entitled to be able to draw a national insurance pension and therefore claimed supplementary benefit (supplementary pension).

The DHSS treated her son as the 'householder' and she as a person in his household. If you look at the main supplementary benefit rates on page 29 you will see that in terms of the November 1977 scale rates she would have received £11.60 a week instead of £14.50 a week. Not only are there different rates for householders and non-householders there is also a different treatment of housing costs (the details of all of the workings of the supplementary benefit system cannot be explored in this pamphlet): a householder receives his full housing costs whereas a non-householder normally receives a 'standard amount' per week, regardless of whether a contribution is made or the amount of the contribution.

In this case the treatment of this lady as a non-householder and the small rent addition combined to give her a low weekly entitlement such as to cause not only hardship to her but hardship to her son who did not earn much.

She appealed to the supplementary benefit appeal tribunal and her status as householder was affirmed. She then received both a higher weekly rate of benefit and her actual housing contribution (half of the housing costs). This was backdated to when she applied. She did not attend her hearing but her son appeared and a representative gave evidence of the nature of the hardship that was being caused by the rigid application of the rules.

In practice there are not many appeals about the scale rates because they are laid down by Parliament; but there can be problems of how to apply the scale rates as is shown in this example.

What are 'exceptional circumstances'?

A widow suffering from a progressive spinal condition was experiencing great financial problems. She was in receipt of an age-related widow's pension and a small addition from the Supplementary Benefits Commission. At the time of contacting the Widows Advisory Service she was in a distraught state because she did not have the money to pay her electricity bill. The Widows Advisory Service helped her out of her immediate difficulty and asked the social services department to negotiate with the DHSS (Supplementary Benefits Commission). She applied for an increase in her weekly benefit. Since the DHSS turned down her application and argued that she had quite sufficient income she appealed (with the social worker's help) to the Supplementary Benefit Appeal Tribunal.

She and her social worker, advised by the WAS, attended the hearing and took along detailed calculations of her weekly expenses. The tribunal awarded her an extra £4 a week, primarily to cover her very high electricity bills (she needed a lot of hot baths and had to use an immersion heater). The tribunal was helped in reaching this decision by a letter from her doctor explaining her condition and her need for warm rooms, hot water, a special diet and for a telephone since she lived alone.

Another widow received an exceptional circumstances addition to meet the cost of bus fares to school for her two daughters; the local education authority had refused to pay because they lived within the 'three mile limit' but the journey to school was, in the mother's and the tribunal's view, too hazardous to be walked or cycled.

What are exceptional needs?

A war widow was faced with a demand for nearly £75 by the Inland Revenue. This was a demand for tax on her pension. Her income at the time (1976) was £17.20 war widow's pension and £7.75 supplementary pension; she lived in a council house and had a son to support. She could not find the £75 out of her weekly income and thus she appealed to the local Supplementary Benefit Appeal Tribunal when the DHSS refused to help. In fact she did not even need to go ahead with attending an appeal hearing because the local DHSS office reviewed the original decision and awarded her an exceptional needs payment to cover the whole cost of her tax bill. (It quite often happens that if you appeal the DHSS will have another look at your case and may give you what you ask for thus enabling you to withdraw your appeal.)

Another widow was faced with a bill of more than £150 to repair some floorboards in her living room. She had only her widow's pension to live on

and could not find the money for this work. She applied to the
Supplementary Benefits Commission (local DHSS office) for help. Her
application was refused. The Widows Advisory Service suggested that she
appeal to the local Supplementary Benefit Appeal Tribunal; this she did and
was not only awarded the cost of this urgent repair but was also given a small
amount of weekly benefit to 'top up' her pension.

Appeals – to the Ombudsmen

Ombudsmen exist to promote good administration. You have the right to
appeal to
– the Parliamentary Commissioner for Administration
– the Commissions for Local Administration
– the Health Service Commissioners
about any matters where, in your view, you think there has been
maladministration.

Y ou appeal to any of the above according to whether the service you want
to complain about is run by central government, local government or the
health authorities.

To appeal to the Parliamentary Commissioner for Administration you
should make a written complaint and sent it to your own M.P. (another M.P.
can take your case but would not normally do so). You should make your
complaint by sending as much detail as possible and any relevant documents.
Y ou can send this to your M.P. at the House of Commons, London SW1. You
must submit your complaint within 12 months of being aggrieved. The
Parliamentary Commissioner will receive and investigate complaints about, for
example, the DHSS, the Inland Revenue, the Department of Employment, the
Department of Education and Science.

To appeal to one of the Commissions for Local Administration you should
write to a local councillor who will then take the matter further. The
Commissions for Local Administration deal with maladministration of services
such as housing, social services, local education, planning. You can get the
names of local councillors from your council's offices or from the Citizens
Advice Bureau.

To appeal to a Health Service Commissioner you apply through your Local
Practitioner Committee within a year of the incident of alleged maladministration. Y ou should send all the details and any relevant documents. The types of
cases dealt with include, bad communications, delays in admission to
hospital, inadequate facilities, and failure to deal with complaints.

Sometimes it is difficult to decide whether what we want to complain
about is maladministration or other matters. For example, a widow who
thinks that her husband was not treated correctly by the doctor would not be
able to make a complaint about maladministration: such a complaint is about
professional competence and judgement.

Decisions of Commissioners rarely bring any direct benefit to the person
who makes the complaint. But other people benefit substantially from
improvements in procedure; one good example of this was that a hospital
failed to give adequate information to a patient about claiming sickness
benefit – the Commissioner's finding of maladministration resulted in the
hospital giving all patients (including emergency admissions) a booklet giving
the necessary advice.

Appeals about Income Tax

You have a right to appeal about your income tax – normally within 30 days
of receiving your Notice of Assessment. You can appeal either by using the
form 64-7(S) which is enclosed with the assessment or by writing to the tax

inspector saying that you want to appeal. You can appeal outside the normal thirty day limit if you can give good reasons for a late appeal.

You should indicate why you are appealing and give any extra information which may be relevant. You should also pay the tax being demanded or apply for a postponement of part or all of the tax.

Usually the tax inspector will come to an agreement with you and your appeal will not have to be heard. However, if the disagreement over your tax liability persists then your appeal will be heard either by the General Commissioners or the Special Commissioners. Most appeals go to the General Commissioners – local non-specialists who are advised by a clerk – who hear appeals locally. There is no legal aid, so any costs you incur have to be borne by you. The Widows Advisory Service may be able to help you to prepare your case without charge.

ORGANIZATIONS

Age Concern, 60 Pitcairn Road, Mitcham, Surrey (01- 640-5431) or 55 Gower Street, London WC2 (01- 637-2886).

Age Concern acts both as a pressure group for those over retirement age and produces useful booklets such as *Help Yourself to Warmth* (50 copies £1.75).

The Child Poverty Action Group, 1 Macklin Street, Drury Lane, London WC2 5NH (01- 242-9149).

CPAG's **Citizens' Rights Office** offers help to all with financial problems. The CRO will provide advice on or, sometimes, representation at, appeal tribunals.

Citizens' Advice Bureaux exist in most parts of the country and offer help and advice to widows as well as other members of the community. Some CAB's have a solicitor on duty at specified times each week. (Headquarters at 26 Bedford Square, London WC1 (01- 637-4066).

Cruse, 6 Lion Gate Gardens, Richmond, Surrey (01- 940-2660).

Both the NAW and Cruse have local branches scattered around the British Isles; they both seek to enhance the social life of widows. Both produce factsheets to help widows. The NAW has set up the Widows Advisory Trust with the purpose of extending advisory services.

Disablement Income Group, Attlee House, Toynbee Hall, 28 Commercial Street, London E1 (01 -247-2128).

DIG is a pressure group for the disabled but also provides an ABC of services and information for disabled people.

Female Financial Advisers, 83 Cambridge Street, London SW1V 4PS (01 -828-5923).

Female Financial Advisers gives help and advice on all money problems, including mortgages. An initial interview and leaflets on managing money and getting a mortgage are free.

Gingerbread, 9 Poland Street, London W1 (01 -737-9014).

The Money Advice Centre, The Birmingham Settlement, 318 Summer Lane, Birmingham B19 (021 -359-3562).

The money advice centre provides expert advice on all financial matters but specializes in debt counselling.

National Association of Widows, Stafford & District Voluntary Services, Chell Road, Stafford (0785 – 45465).

The National Council for One-Parent Families, 255 Kentish Town, London NW5 (01 -267-1361).

Both Gingerbread and the National Council for One-Parent Families help all one-parent families, the separated, divorced, unmarried mothers, widowers.

The Parliamentary All-Party Group for Widows and One-Parent Families, The House of Commons, London (Chairman: Tony Durant, MP).

She Can Do It, c/o A Woman's Place, 38 Earlham Street, London WC2 (01 -836-6081).

A register of women with skills to offer – electricians, plumbers, decorators, gardeners, baby-sitters, translators, typists etc is kept at A Woman's Place. If you would rather hire a woman than a man or if you have skills to offer get in touch. At the moment the network is restricted to the London area. The workshop also can put you in touch with a female removal team in the London area.

Shelter Housing Aid Centre, 189a Old Brompton Road, London SW5 (01 373-7276).

Shelter Housing Aid Centre gives advice and help on all housing problems but specializes in homelessness and threatened eviction.

Women's Release, 1 Elgin Avenue, London W9 3PR (01 -289-1123 or in emergency outside office hours 01-603-8654).

Women's Release gives help and advice to women on legal and welfare rights problems.

Women's Rights Centre, c/o North Kensington Law Centre, 74 Golbourne Road, London W10 (01-969-7473).

In the Women's Rights Centre women give legal advice to women, help to find sympathetic solicitors and help with obtaining legal aid.

BOOKS AND PAMPHLETS

There is a wide range of books and pamphlets which are useful to widows. A selection of these is listed below.

Anna Coote & Tess Gill, *Women's Rights: A Practical Guide*, Penguin 1978, £1.25

Gordon Cummings, *The Complete Guide to Investment*, Penguin 1970, 75p

Daily Mail, *Income Tax Guide*, (revised annually), about 60p

Dennis Marsden, *Mother's Alone: Poverty and the Fatherless Family*, Penguin 1973, 70p

Sheila Moore, *Working for Free*, Pan 1976, 95p

C. Murray-Parkes, *Bereavement: Studies of Grief in Adult Life*, Penguin 1975, 80p

Lily Pincus, *Death and the Family: Importance of Mourning*, Faber 1976, £4.50

The Reader's Digest produces a *Complete Do-It-Yourself Manual*, 1974, £7.40. A cheaper Do-It-Yourself Home Maintenance and Repairs by Alan Taylor is available at £1.75.

Edith Rudinger, *What to Do When Someone Dies*. Consumer's Association 1974. £1.50 The Consumer's Association produces a number of other very useful short books covering, for example, taxation, good purchases, electricity supply and safety. For details, write to the Consumer's Association, 14 Buckingham Street, London WC2. Most public libraries have them too.

Mary Stott, *Forgetting's No Excuse*, Virago 1975, £1.75

Carolyn Faulder, Christine Jackson, Mary Lewis, *The Women's Directory*, Virago 1976, £1.95

DEPARTMENT OF HEALTH AND SOCIAL SECURITY LEAFLETS

The DHSS issues many leaflets, free of charge, which are designed to give guidance as to entitlement to the many benefits available under the National Insurance, Supplementary Benefits and other income maintenace schemes. The following is a list of those found to be most useful to widows.

NI 51 National Insurance Guide for Widows
NI 51E National Insurance Guidance for Recently Widowed Women
NI 49 Death Grant
NI 13 Widows Benefit
NI 10 Industrial Death Benefit for widows and other dependants
MPL 147 War Widows – Officers
MPL 148 War Widows – Other Ranks and Civilians
NI 51C Age Related Widow's Pensions
NI 15A Retirement Pensions for Widows
NI 15 Your Retirement Pension
NI 92 Earning Extra Pension by Cancelling Your Retirement

NI 9 How a Stay in Hospital can affect your Social Security Benefit
NI 48 Late Paid or Unpaid Contributions: their Effect upon Benefits

NI 196 Social Security Benefit Rates

FIS 1* Family Income Supplement
SB 1* Supplementary Benefits – Pensions and Allowances
SL 8 Supplementary Allowances for People Registering as Unemployed
SL 11 How your Savings and Capital affect your Supplementary Pension
M 11* Free Dental Treatment, glasses, prescriptions, milk and vitamins
MV 1 Milk and Vitamins for you and your Children
H 11 Help with Travelling for Hospital Patients
OC 2 Supplementary Benefits – Help with Heating Costs

NI 210 Non-contributory Invalidity Pension
NI 212 Invalid Care Allowance
HB 1 Help for Handicapped People
NI 205 Attendance Allowance
NI 211 Mobility Allowance
NI 184 Pensions for People over 80

FB 1 is a booklet which describes 'Family Benefits and Pensions'. It gives a brief guide to the benefits mentioned above and to several others such as child's special allowance, guardian's allowance etc. It can be obtained free from local or regional offices of the DHSS and is invaluable. (Since only a limited number are printed you may have to wait some time for your copy.)

The leaflets marked * can be obtained from both local post offices and from DHSS offices; the remainder are usually only obtainable from the DHSS.